Katharine Weeting

Emyl Jenkins'
Southern Hospitality

EMYL JENKINS'

Southern Hospitality

Never will surpass
Curt and Kathy's
Northern Hospitality
But we're waiting
to share our new life with you

PHOTOGRAPHS BY WALTER SMALLING, JR.

Merry
Christmas '95
Isabel and Bob

CROWN PUBLISHERS, INC.   NEW YORK

To Charles Kuralt

Whose mellow voice and timeless words
capture the spirit of the South like none other.

and Langdon and Joslin

My Southern children named for their Northern ancestors.

To my many friends

It's unusual for a writer to be at a loss for words, but when I sat down to write
the acknowledgments—such a formal word for a heartfelt thank you— I truly did not know
where to begin, or where to end. Then when leafing through my notes of pages and pages of
names of all the sharing people who helped make *Southern Hospitality* possible, I threw up my
hands in frustration. It is no exaggeration to say that hundreds of people contributed to
these pages. Actually that's probably an understatement, for literally everyone I met over
the phone, through the mails and faxes, and in person contributed not just information,
suggestions, hints and tips, but showed me the secret to true Southern hospitality—
giving your best. *You* are Southern hospitality! Thank you.

Passages from Marjorie Kinnan Rawlings's writings are reprinted with the
permission of Macmillan Publishing. In some cases, the author has searched diligently
to find sources and to obtain specific permission to use them, without success.

Published by Crown Publishers, Inc., 201 East 50th Street, New York,
New York 10022. Member of the Crown Publishing Group.

Random House, Inc. New York, Toronto, London, Sydney, Auckland

CROWN is a trademark of Crown Publishers, Inc.

Manufactured in China.

LIBRARY OF CONGRESS CATALOGING-IN-PUBLICATION DATA
Jenkins, Emyl.
[Southern Hospitality]
Emyl Jenkins' Southern hospitality.—1st ed.
Includes index.
1. Southern States—Social life and customs—1865
2. Hospitality—Southern States. I. Title. II. Title: Southern hospitality.
F216.2.J38 1994
975—dc20   94-1188
CIP

ISBN 0-517-59477-3

10 9 8 7 6 5 4 3 2 1

FIRST EDITION

$\mathscr{C}$ontents

If a man be gracious to strangers, it shows that he is a citizen of the world, and his heart is no island, cut off from other islands, but a continent that joins them.

Sir Francis Bacon, 1561–1626

Southern Hospitality

Ah . . . Southern hospitality. The phrase needs no explanation. Everyone everywhere, it seems, intuitively knows what Southern hospitality means. ⌒ It pops up in the most unexpected places, like that day my morning newspaper interview ran into the afternoon. If I was going to get from Richmond, Virginia, to Raleigh, North Carolina, in time for my late-afternoon appointment, I could forget lunch. ⌒ But luck was with me. At the entrance to a parking lot on East Main Street stood one of those hurdy-gurdy–style lunch carts. Its oversize makeshift menu plopped sideways at one corner of the wagon caught

Streams of sun through an open door in Maryland remind us of what Southerners do best— welcome others into their homes and lives for gracious hospitality.

My hunger rose as my hopes fell. "You can't eat a salad and drive at the same time," I complained. "Alfalfa sprouts, marinated artichokes, and sun-dried tomatoes just don't make it from the lap to the mouth when you're whizzing down I-85 caught in the middle lane of sixty-five-mile-an-hour traffic."

"But we do have some French bread," she quickly offered, politely ignoring my sarcastic quip. "Would some chicken salad on French bread work? I could make that for you."

"Why, that would be wonderful!" I exclaimed, taking her up on her offer. "Would it be too much trouble?"

"Of course not." She smiled back at me, already beginning to slice the bread. "That's what Southern hospitality is all about."

She's right. Ever since colonial days, visitors to the South have sung the praises of the gracious Southern people. The old books and journals are filled with stories of warmth, kindnesses, gentleness, and generosity encountered from Maryland to Mississippi.

Why, long before thoughts of the Revolutionary War were circulating, an eighteenth-century English traveler wrote home that "The Virginians are generous, extremely hospitable, and possess very liberal sentiments." Furthermore, he added that the idea of "general hospitality" was found throughout "all the Southern provinces."

It really must have been true, because in 1705 Robert Beverly wrote that strangers traveling the Virginia back roads could stop at any gentleman's, planter's, or "good Housekeeper's" home and be offered a bed, even if the host had to sit up all night "to make room for a weary Traveller to repose himself after his journey."

A century later Southern hospitality was

my eye. Nouvelle cuisine selections were scribbled in green and pink chalk. I skipped the soups and was making my way through the salads when a young woman, her gentle drawl barely audible above the rush-hour traffic, asked "May I help you?"

"Yes . . . I'll take a, ah . . . sandwich . . . of, ah, some sort," I stuttered indecisively.

"I'm afraid we only have soups and salads," she answered apologetically.

never more evident than at Thomas Jefferson's home, Monticello. In those days visitors often stayed for days and weeks at a time. George Ticknor, a young Harvard-educated Boston lawyer, described how, as he was preparing to leave, Mr. Jefferson begged him to stay longer. Jefferson even implored Ticknor to let him send his horse away. It was only when Jefferson found his guest "resolved on going" that he relented. Then Jefferson "bade us farewell in the heartiest style of Southern hospitality."

So it is little wonder that Thomas Cooper De Leon, in his 1907 book *Belles, Beaux and Brains of the 60s*, fondly recalled "That pleasantry of courtesy, 'This house and all it contains is yours,' came nearer realization in Old Virginia than anywhere on the globe. . . . Hospitality is like 'mercy' as described by Portia," De Leon wrote. " 'It blesses him that give and him that takes.' And this the host of the rare old Dominion knew and practiced."

But these days, in our self-absorbed world, few people even take the time to give compliments anymore, to say nothing of keeping alive gentle traditions and remembering to practice good manners. Yet I had just enjoyed the good feeling that comes when a little Southern hospitality was generously served up at a sidewalk lunch cart.

After leaving Richmond, once I had maneuvered my way through city traffic and was safely on that long, lonesome stretch of interstate highway that runs from Petersburg, Virginia, to Henderson, North Carolina, I reached for my sandwich. Suddenly I had a grand idea.

Wouldn't it be fun to travel through the South to savor the tradition of Southern hospitality that since long ago was the standard

of kindness and unreserved friendliness? I had traveled from one end of that grand land to the other for two years straight—once to chronicle my book *Southern Christmas* and again share my wonderful experiences and discoveries with others through radio, TV, and talks. Still, those trips only made me all the more eager to return to the South, over and over. I now knew the places I had yet to see—the riches I had yet to discover. As John

At The Elms, a late eighteenth century home in Natchez, cotton balls are as lovely as any bouquet of white roses.

A collage of scenes captured during my travels speaks of the interwoven pleasures of food and conviviality as celebrated across the South.

Steinbeck said, "A journey is a person in itself; no two are alike."

Perhaps I was inspired by the way the long winter shadows fell on the thick stand of yellow pine trees that lined the road as I whizzed by. Or maybe it was the way the afternoon sun turned the winter wheat a golden brown in the far-distant fields. But I was captivated by the idea, and my thoughts wandered back to my own Southern childhood.

The many faces of the South reflect the rich diversity of its traditions, customs, and pastimes. There's the Strawberry Festival in Plant City, Florida (above), dinner at Mrs. Wilkes in Savannah, Georgia (right) and Mardi Gras in Mobile, Alabama (below).

I've been told that I instinctively knew all about Southern hospitality by the time I was three. That was the summer of 1944. Daddy was a naval officer in Europe during those World War II years, and Mother and I were temporarily living with her parents in Raleigh. Early one morning Mother and I boarded the train and traveled all the way to Boston and then on to Webster, Massachusetts, my father's hometown, to visit Grandmother Joslin.

My New England grandmother was a tall, stately woman with a clipped Boston accent. She was so proper that everyone, even her own daughter-in-law, called her Mrs. Joslin. Though I loved her dearly, she was a formidable lady. Of course I don't remember much about that visit of so long ago, but my mother oftentimes has told me about the luncheon given by Mrs. Shaw, Grandmother Joslin's best friend and an equally staid New Englander.

We ate outside on that mild Massachusetts late June day. Dainty finger sandwiches

and marinated cucumbers and tomatoes were served on pressed glass plates. On the center of the table was an antique milkglass bowl filled with stylishly arranged summer garden greens. It was surely a lovely occasion. Mother tells me that everything went well (which means I behaved myself), until we were saying our good-byes.

At that point I chirped up in my little-girl voice, "Mrs. Shaw, down South when my mamma [my Southern grandmother] has a party she doesn't pick turnip greens. She puts *flowers* on the table!"

I smiled to myself. Why, I hadn't thought

about Mrs. Shaw and my first trip to Massachusetts in some forty years, yet now I could think of nothing else.

Southern hospitality. What a ring the phrase has to it. How inviting and refreshing.

But what makes it so? "What makes *Southern* hospitality so special?" my *Yankee* voice asked. After all, as the child of a Northern father with such ancestors as the Langdons, Joslins, and Hurlbuts, I can't just ignore my Yankee heritage, of which I'm boastfully proud. Yet because I *am* part Southerner and

part Northerner I know the difference.

When it comes right down to it, Southern hospitality is born of a unique lifestyle—one of grace and style laced with a deep appreciation for leisure and laughter. Southern hospitality is a blend of many honorable virtues that have been passed down through the generations—gentleness, kindness, the receiving of strangers and friends alike with openness, selflessness, and caring.

Southern hospitality is the gentle art of sharing. It is the noble gesture of putting another's comfort before your own. It is taking the time to make others feel good about themselves. And when you're on the receiving end, a liberal dousing of Southern hospitality makes you feel cared for and important. It can even fill you with confidence.

Once again I heard my North Carolina–born and bred mother's voice echoing out of the past. So many times she said to me, "Southern hospitality is nothing more than good manners." Yes, but it is more, really. Today, like long ago, Southern hospitality brings moments of joy, delight, and pleasantness to our days, and a richness to the quality of our lives.

It *would* be fun to chronicle it all—past and present, I kept thinking. Now what would I need?

First, a book contract. (I got that.) Then a photographer with a vagabond spirit to match my own. (I found that soulmate.) And time.(I would make that.) I already had a library full of old books—and a new atlas of the southeastern United States. In no time at

In Nashville, Tennessee, employees of The Union Station Hotel celebrate a "Turn of the Century Gala" in period dress (above), while in the deep South, oysters are served at Uglesich's in New Orleans (left) and recollections of the old country are exchanged in Tampa's historic Ybor City (below).

Hospitality: A Timeless Virtue

Roman mythology tells us that true hospitality began in the ancient land of Phrygia, where the townspeople had become selfish and mean. When strangers sought rest and shelter in the village, they were chased away, pelted with rocks and sticks.

When Jupiter, the protector of travelers in strange lands, and his son, Mercury, heard of this, they disguised themselves as weary travelers and visited Phrygia. True enough, they were rudely and cruelly turned away again and again. Finally, at the very poorest hut in the land, they were welcomed by a gentle, aged couple, Baucis and Philemon.

Together this loving wife and husband gave these disguised gods the best they had to offer, humble though it was—shelter, food, and comforting friendship.

Only when the wine pitcher was never empty and their bowls were always full, no matter how much their guests drank and ate, did the hosts realize these travelers were divine. As was customary in myths, Jupiter and Mercury flooded the town to punish the selfish people of Phrygia. And they blessed the selfless couple by turning their tiny home into a grand temple. There Baucis and Philemon lived as priestess and priest, showering hospitality upon all who happened by.

But the couple had asked for one favor from Jupiter and Mercury. They said that they had been so happy in their marriage that they wished to die together.

According to the legend, that time came one day as Baucis and Philemon sat at their door, peacefully watching the sun set. Together their spirits left the earth, but their bodies were turned into two trees that sprang from one trunk—trees joined in a loving embrace, forever entwined.

How often I remembered this legend while traveling through the South as I sipped wine from always-full pitchers, feasted abundantly, and enjoyed the comfort of glowing fires and giving hearts. Hospitality and love have always gone together. I have even remarked that Southern hospitality began the day Pocahontas selflessly threw her body over John Smith to save his life.

My Florida friend Cookie O'Brien begs to differ. She says it all began in St. Augustine on September 8, 1565, when Pedro Menendez and the men aboard the *Adelanteado* disembarked and were welcomed by friendly Indians.

Ancient Spanish books tell us that first the explorers gave the Indians gifts from Europe—clothing, beads, mirrors, scissors, knives, and other trifles—then they dined.

The Spaniards had brought many foods with them on their journey—cheese, wine, salt, flour, hardtack, bacon, dried figs and raisins, codfish, garlic, marmalade, chickpeas, even oil, vinegar, honey, and confections. Likewise the Indians shared their food—raw, boiled, and roasted fish and oysters, and, of course, maize. Together they shared their food around a table "set with tablecloths and napkins," thus celebrating America's first Thanksgiving.

But if you visit Virginia's Berkeley Plantation on the James River you will learn that the first official *English-speaking* Thanksgiving was held *there* in 1619, two years before the better-known 1621 celebration at Plymouth, Massachusetts. It seems that even before the tiny, good ship *Margaret* left England with thirty-eight passengers and eight crew members, orders had been written that upon landing they would give thanks with a prayer service. Now on the first Sunday in November an annual Virginia Thanksgiving Festival is held at Berkeley.

Florida, Virginia, Massachusetts? What does it matter? Hospitality, like all of life's most important values, cannot be traced to one time, one event, one country, or one culture. What is essential is that it be continued.

all I was, as we say in the South, ready to head on down the road.

I had met Walter Smalling, my exceptionally handsome, high-spirited photographer, only twice before. Our third meeting was on February 7, 1993, when we packed the car to the gills and pulled out from the Virginia suburbs of Washington on the first phase of our grand adventure.

The first leg of the trip would keep us on the road for a month and a day—quite a stretch of time to spend in close company with someone you have met just twice, once for an introductory chat over a glass of wine and once for lunch in a Chinese restaurant. But I knew all would be fine when, over a spicy dish of Szechuan beef, Walter set forth the first rule of our proposed venture. It went something like this: When you've got a brainstorm of an idea that can't wait, it's all right to talk with your mouth full. We haven't had a quiet moment since.

How could we be silent when there is so much to see, to enjoy, to behold, to exclaim over, to chat about, when we're experiencing the beauty, the variety, the *hospitality* of the South! We found it everywhere we ventured . . . from sleepy little Columbus, Georgia, to touristy, but always enchanting, Charleston, South Carolina.

Southern hospitality was as evident at the down-at-the-heels motel in Lacoochee, Florida, as it was at the breathtakingly elegant Breakers in ritzy Palm Beach. We felt equally welcomed in the crowded halls of the Vanderbilts' glorious North Carolina Biltmore Estate and at Fort Hill, John C. Calhoun's little-known South Carolina home. And most important of all, people everywhere openly shared their stories of Southern hospitality

with us—from Julie Grimes at the Virginia Department of Tourism, whom I never met but who couldn't do enough for us, to the Yankee pilgrims we journeyed with aboard the famed *Mississippi Queen* who searched us out when they heard about our project.

Our only disappointment came when we ran out of time and, eventually, money! How Walter and I hated to leave each place we visited. How we hated to have to pass by the hamlets and homes that we knew held rich, endearing stories. We never once became travel-weary or homesick, even at 3 A.M. on March 1 when we could find no empty rooms in central Florida. While singing Southern country melodies to keep one another awake, we began enthusiastically planning our next project to bring us South again. But that's for another day.

Come with us now. Come see the sunny South. Come learn a little about our history while you capture the joy, the festivity, and the pleasures of this part of our country often lovingly called "the Southern part of Heaven." Come sample the foods, enjoy the stories,

When my daughter, Joslin, joined us for a day of photographing Virginia plantations, we ventured out to see Shirley as eighteenth-century visitors would have from the James River.

catch the joie de vivre, and celebrate the ever-seductive mood of this beautiful land, its colorful folk, charming ways, and enduring traditions that all add up to Southern hospitality. Come to the South where life still moves at a leisurely pace and there's always time for the graceful art of savoring life.

But, like all the best things in life, there is a secret to getting the most from Southern hospitality—the same secret that the travelers and adventurers of so long ago learned. You must cast your cares aside. You must forget the pressures of the modern world that consume your time and burden your soul. You must, in the true sense of living, dive right in!

The ever-inviting Southern scene— the welcoming front porch of a charming historic home bathed in late afternoon sunlight.

If you haven't been South before, come on in and sit a spell!

And if you have, come on back. We're mighty glad you came.

~

"You ought to do your best. They are so generous and hospitable, and so unconscious of any merit, or exceptional credit, in the matter of hospitality."
Mr. Brewster of Texas, agreeing with Mary Boykin Chesnut as she plans parties to return the "hospitalities of this most hospitable people" of Richmond in January 1864.

Dolley Madison

A QUEEN OF HEARTS

~

"Pizzazz" was not an eighteenth-century word. But Dolley Madison had it, along with style, grace, and charm. With sparkling blue eyes, dark curly hair, rouged cheeks, and a whimsical spirit to match, this Virginia-born hostess brought generous, fun-loving hospitality to our nation's capital. Indeed, if gentle Baucis and Philemon exemplify universal hospitality, ever-gracious Dolley Madison epitomizes *Southern* hospitality.

Dolley Madison, wife of James Madison, our fourth President and the "Father of the Constitution," was a vivid contrast to her immediate predecessor, Abigail Adams, John Adams' stern, strict, New England wife. Because Thomas Jefferson was widowed, when James Madison served as vice president, Dolley occasionally acted as the nation's hostess, often having one party after the other. Once she became First Lady, the White House literally was "crowded with company from top to bottom."

According to Conover Hunt, author of two books about the Madisons, Dolley Madison was a genius at soothing tensions, the true earmark of a great hostess in any era.

But Dolley Madison was much more than just an exceptionally able hostess. Her illustrious life was filled with so many remarkable accomplishments.

First, in 1809, she hosted the immensely popular White House "Wednesday drawing rooms," a social gathering that lasted from twilight till around nine. In *The President's House*, historian William Seale writes "Guests moved about freely through the suite; they clustered in small groups to talk. To a political population often bored with small-town life, James and Dolley Madison gave a hearty and elegant time."

And her biographers enjoy describing the bountiful, overflowing "Southern" tables Dolley prepared for her guests—the same spreads that the British foreign minister and his wife criticized as being "more like harvest-home suppers" than appropriate fare in the President's home!

When the British burned Washington and the White House on August 24, 1814, Dolley Madison valiantly saved invaluable official papers and maps and, at the last minute, Washington's portrait. Yet the press assailed Dolley Madison, contending that had she stayed, she could have saved the White House itself. Unable to return to the charred White House, the Madisons moved to the Octagon House, where Dolley attempted to restore festivity and graciousness to the humiliated city. But her efforts failed, and upon Madison's retirement they returned to Montpelier, their Orange County, Virginia, home.

Long before Dolley Madison's fortunes turned, it was written that "Mrs. Madison's conduct would be graced by propriety were she placed in the most adverse circumstances in life." Dolley Madison lived out this prophecy in her last years, when "her sunshiny disposition never left her, and she went to her grave with a word of kindness and encouragement for everyone she knew."

But there is more. These days, when women are making so many worthwhile contributions, we should remember that Dolley Madison helped blaze the way. She took women to Congress to watch "law in action," an act that led to an unprecedented congressional declaration: "Whenever it shall be [Mrs. Madison's] pleasure to visit the House she be requested to take a seat within the Hall."

In 1912 Edith Tunis Sale wrote "Even as an old lady—if one can ever think of her as old—her girlish laugh and gentle voice swayed some political destinies, and when she died in 1849 she left a place and space in life that must remain for always unfilled."

Her faithful admirers agreed, for Dolley Madison was given a state funeral in Washington, with "the largest funeral procession yet seen in the city."

Dolley Madison, who tirelessly upheld and shared the rich tradition of Southern hospitality through her life for all to enjoy, undoubtedly would have loved it—and thrown a grand party to boot!

Pine Apple, Alabama

Driving through the sky. That's how Mother described those vast, interminably boring stretches of interstate highway.

After seemingly endless hours of seeing only dense stands of tall pine trees and the usual highway directional signs, Walter and I were ready for a back country road. Trouble was, we were running late.

"Are we *ever* going to get to Mobile?" I hinted out loud, wishing he'd go just a little faster. A few miles later I tried again. "We've got to check in, unpack, and meet John Peebles (our host for the Mardi Gras festivities) before the parade."

Despite my repeated urgings, Walter turned a deaf ear. Then, suddenly without any warning, and not much slowing down, he swerved the car *off* of Interstate 65 onto Alabama State Highway 10 heading northwest. We were supposed to be going south.

"Where are we going?" I asked incredulously.

"Pine Apple." Walter grinned without flinching.

"Pineapple?"

Pine Apple, Alabama, proudly boasts its heritage and its name—the universal symbol for hospitality.

"No, Pine Apple. Just wait."

"What for?" I wondered, but instead I muttered "Oh." I didn't protest because almost immediately the scenery was as lovely as the early spring day. Newly budded maples and spring-flowering fruit trees dotted the open fields. Even the ubiquitous pine trees seemed more graceful, more stately, like dark columns silhouetted against the cornflower-blue sky. It was, in the fullest sense of the word, wonderfully refreshing.

We had traveled only a mile or so when we came upon the prettiest little late-Victorian cottage you can imagine, set back from the road in a grove of sycamore trees. The house was stuck in the middle of nowhere, but the quaint gingerbread work on its graceful wrap-around porch was as lacy and intricate as that found on the finest, most attractive homes in Pass Christian, Mississippi, or in New Orleans' Garden District. When a red fox scurried in front of our path and disappeared into a thicket of wind-swept daffodils that lined the curving road, I knew many enjoyable miles lay ahead on this unscheduled adventure.

"No one ever told me how beautiful rural Alabama is," Walter said as we stopped time after time at the slightest whim—sometimes to take a picture and sometimes just to enjoy the scene. Nor does any travel book extol the charm of our destination—once booming, but now almost forgotten, Pine Apple, the town originally named "Friendship."

Pine Apple was settled by "Easterners" from the Carolinas, Georgia, and Virginia around 1820 and named "Friendship." But there was already another Friendship, Alabama, and that one had a post office.

So the settlers named their town in honor of the pine and apple trees that gave the land its beauty and the town its wealth. Pine trees were cut for timber and the apple harvest was turned into cider.

Through the end of the 1800s new businesses and more settlers were attracted to Pine Apple. Today impressive nineteenth-century homes along the now lightly traveled main street of this peaceful hamlet reflect this era of prosperity and history. But things change.

With the dawning of the twentieth century, businesses and people moved to other towns. Newly built major highways skirted around Pine Apple. And so like Sweet Auburn, Goldsmith's deserted village, this little Southern town remains much the way it was almost a century ago, as pretty as a movie set frozen in time.

I learned the history of Pine Apple from Kenneth Barlow, the town's postal clerk, a friendly man full of smiles and good humor who told me, "We don't get many writers and photographers coming through here."

His comment didn't surprise me. In fact, as Walter and I slowly wandered along the cheerful, postcard-pretty streets, I asked him, "Just how *did* you know to come here?"

"Any place named Pine Apple has to be charming and friendly." He shrugged as if to say that's just how things work out.

"Serendipity," I smiled back.

Walter's right—that's just how things are in the South.

Anyway, these days the town's name is as often written "Pineapple" as it is Pine Apple. That seems most appropriate for a settlement that was first called "Friendship," for, as everyone knows, the pineapple is the universal symbol of hospitality.

We repacked our gear, climbed into the car, and headed back toward Interstate 10. Amazingly, the rest of the trip seemed to just whiz along.

Looking back, I wouldn't take anything for our detour to Pine Apple. I thought of that little town recently when I came upon this passage written in 1916 by a New Yorker, Louise Hale, after she and her photographer husband (also named Walter), chronicled their journey through Virginia.

"When the way is bad lift your head and hear the mocking bird; turn your head and see the beauty about you. Look to the people and the road will be easier by the smile they give to you. It is unending—and takes no toll."

That's just what we did that day. And guess what? We made it to Mobile in plenty of time.

Today the hamlet is quiet—a whisper of an earlier, bustling, time—but Pine Apple's undaunted spirit is visible everywhere.

From centerpieces
to bedposts, from
Christmas decora-
tions to fanciful
finials, the ever-
welcoming pineapple
invites one and all to
enjoy Southern
hospitality.

Unconquerable Hearts

Many traditional Southern ways of life changed with the coming of the War Between the States. Men were away at battle; the fine foods and wines the Southerners loved were difficult and sometimes impossible to obtain; grand homes and furnishing were destroyed. During those war years, and even later, many colorful Southern festivities—fox hunting, the riding tournaments, Mardi Gras—were only memories.

Yet wonderful stories of Southern hospitality come from those tragic years. Many are heartwarming stories that reach across all political or warring factions and speak of humankind's true, loving hospitality.

Other stories tell of dances and parties, dinners and galas that were held in spite of the battles being waged. Mary Boykin Chesnut's famed *Diary from Dixie* is filled with descriptions of war-year dinner parties and social visits. Through her writings we watch the years pass and conditions worsen.

In an entry on May 1862 she describes Columbia, South Carolina, as "the place for good living, pleasant people, pleasant dinners, pleasant drives. I feel

Varina Howell Davis (pictured below) epitomized Southern graciousness in the brightest and the darkest days of the South.

that I have put the dinner in the wrong place. They are the climax of the good things here. This is the most hospitable place in the world, and the dinners are worthy of it. . . ."

But time and the war brought vast changes. Reading along, three years later in April 1865, we learn how Southerners have fallen upon a new device. "We keep a cookery book on the mantelpiece, and when our dinner is deficient, we just read a pudding, or a creme. It does not entirely satisfy the appetite, this dessert in imagination, but perhaps it is as good for the digestion." Good humor adds immeasurably to a hospitable spirit.

If Dolley Madison took Southern hospitality to the nation's capital, Mrs. Jefferson Davis kept its spirit alive as the First Lady of the Confederacy.

Varina Howell Davis of Natchez, Mississippi, was an accomplished writer whose books were published and read worldwide. Descended from a fine family—her grandfather, Richard Howell, fought in the Revolution and was Governor of New Jersey—she even wrote an etiquette book. In her youth, Varina was acclaimed as a fine Washington hostess during the years that Jefferson Davis served as a Mississippi congressman, then senator, and as secretary of war under President Pierce.

Varina Jefferson's very sad later years were spent in much reduced circumstances at Beauvoir on the Gulf Coast of Mississippi. There, family tragedy, near poverty, the death of children, and her husband's failing health consumed her time and energy. Yet it was said that Mrs. Davis never failed to "make a show drawing on a modest outlay."

During the 1870s Jefferson Davis was so revered that people made pilgrimages to Beauvoir to pay him homage. Davis steadfastly refused money gifts, but he felt it would be rude not to at least offer these uninvited guests some refreshments. The story goes that in the predawn hours the Davises' hospitable friends and neighbors left fruits, vegetables, and other food gifts on the steps of Beauvoir.

But Christmas, the celebration that Southerners made merry, called for the greatest extravagance. S. N. Dahlgren's 1877 account is so descriptive and spirited that I include it here.

I must tell you first about our . . . "Bill of fare." First oysters, raw, on the half shell just from the Ocean, then oyster soup, next roast turkey, roast mutton, roast beef, a fine ham, fried oysters, salmon, crabs, sweet potatoes, Irish potatoes, rice, onions, celery, cranberry-sauce, jelly, etc., etc., with plenty of claret and sherry. After this the table was cleared of everything, and the most beautifully arranged dish I ever saw before was brought in by two men on a large silver salver four feet long by three feet wide was a magnificent peacock (which had been skinned so as to preserve the beautiful feathers perfectly; the longest of which measured five feet; and then arranged as if alive) upon whose back and extended wings a dish rested, in which was the peacock, nicely roasted and stuffed with oysters etc. This is a dish that is rarely ever prepared except for kings. After this several sorts of desserts were brought on. . . . Next oranges, Dutch cheese and crackers and lastly coffee. Our guests on this occasion were President Davis, Genl. Jubal H. Early, and Genl. J. R. Davis. Christmas night we give a grand reception in honour of Genl. Early. All the distinguished persons in this section of the country were present with their wives and fair daughters. The whole yard was lit up with reflectors.

While the house was a blaze of light, cheerful pine fires burned on every hearth; while hundreds of wax candles from the grand old chandelier showered a flood of variegated light upon the happy throng of gallant gentlemen and beautiful women, only to be reflected back by the sparkling eyes and brilliant gems upon the necks and fingers of their fair owners. Just before the entertainment broke up, which was next morning, the old Virginia Reel was proposed and everybody joined in, old and young. Even Jefferson Davis, Genl. Early, Genl. Davis, Maj. Wolthall, Judge Henderson, Dr. Hollingsworth and many others. The above named gentlemen had not danced before for twenty years, and none of them are under sixty five or seventy. Such a scene will never be witnessed again. During the course of the evening I was called upon for a toast, and as the head of the house I had to say one; so I immediately drank the following impromptu one, which caused a great deal of amusement and laughter. "Here's to that honoured commander, who was always early upon the field of battle, whose name was written early upon the hearts of his countrymen; may he be early restored to his former hospitality, and never be late at Christmas reception."

Reading the toast so spontaneously delivered at a good time in the midst of bad times, I drank this toast: May we all keep Southern hospitality alive throughout the year.

Jefferson Davis signed his last document as the President of the Confederacy at the Sutherlin home. He later wrote to the people of Danville, Virginia, thanking them for their Southern hospitality.

Memorial Day Parade

*"Confederates who came home from
the war spent the rest of their lifetime telling
their children about the men who had died
for the South in the Civil War."*
Ben Robertson, *Red Hills and Cotton*

When my mother (who at this writing is eighty-eight years old) was a little girl, she lived in downtown Raleigh, North Carolina. Anytime, but especially on Sunday afternoons, it was fashionable to promenade around the imposing State Capitol Building—the Capitol Square, as it was known.

Back in the 1910s, the aging Confederate soldiers gathered under the shady oak trees and told their stories to all who would listen. That was my mother's heritage and she held it dear. I grew up hearing those oral-history stories told secondhand. I have forgotten most of them, but not this one, for, as Walter said when I told him the tale, "It ought to be true even if it isn't."

Memorial Day was a state holiday—a parade day that everyone took part in. It began when ROTC cadets solemnly led the grand procession from the college campus to Union Cemetery—all the way across town. There schoolchildren placed flowers they had brought from their gardens on each soldier's grave, those of the Union and the Confederate dead alike. Then they and their families picnicked in the graveyard on this day of remembrance of those who gave their lives for the "lost, noble cause."

Our story begins when a young ROTC commander was sent from the North to North Carolina Agriculture and Mechanics College, as North Carolina State University was then named. His beautiful wife had social aspirations, but,

being a Yankee, she was scorned by the Southern matriarchs who ruled the town.

During his first spring in Raleigh a committee of those very women his wife so badly hoped to be accepted by called upon the commander. Theirs was a simple request.

"Do not fly the American flag," the Southern women—widows, mothers, and daughters of Confederate soldiers—beseeched the young Northerner. "Let only our grand Bonnie Blue flag fly."

Then, as they were leaving, the grand dame of the group turned and added, "Oh yes, please remember us to your lovely wife. We're having a tea next week and we thought she might like to come."

The commander was distraught. His one chance to please his wife would make him go against his duty. All night long he agonized over his decision.

The dawn brought a glorious, cloudless late-spring Southern day—the perfect day for the parade, the ceremony, and the picnic. Townsfolk, Confederate veterans, college students, families, and children began gathering for their long, slow procession down Hillsborough Street—past the Grove at Saint Mary's College where the Union troops had camped in 1864, in front of the Capitol Square, finally ending at Union Cemetery.

When everyone was in place the signal was given, the drums rolled. Deafening, wild Rebel yells erupted as, with great flourish, the color guard unfurled the Bonnie Blue flag and the parade began.

That day the Stars and Bars proudly waved in the breeze, brightly gleamed in the sun. She was a glorious sight to the throngs of Southerners who lined the streets of Raleigh. The American flag remained tightly and securely bound through the entire day.

How did this happen? Outside the ROTC room the Yankee commander had posted an official notice: "Due to the fear of inclement weather, the Stars and Stripes must not be flown today."

From sun-warmed solariums in Delaware to sun-kissed gardens of the deep South, the beautiful, colorful camellia blossoms that brighten Southern homes during the winter months are without equal. These camellias (right) are from Alabama's famed Bellingrath Gardens.

"I never saw prettier, more lovely, or better-tempered girls any-where—mostly from Virginia and Maryland." Sir Augustus Foster, attaché to the British Prime Minister, upon attending a ball in Washington in 1805

We Southerners are, of course, a mythological people. Supposed to dwell in moonlight

or incandescence, we are in part to blame for our own legendary character.

JONATHAN DANIELS, A SOUTHERNER DISCOVERS THE SOUTH

Southern Traditions and Celebrations

Nothing is as exciting as a book tour, and for this Southerner, presenting my book *Southern Christmas* at Macy's in Herald Square was a grown-up dream come true. Natalie Wood seated on Santa's lap in *Miracle on 34th Street* could not have been any more thrilled to be there than I was. Trouble is, there's seldom time to savor these once-in-a-lifetime experiences. That December day was no different. To be sure that I would make my plane to the next city, a Macy's executive rushed me downstairs to a waiting cab. ⌐ "Take her to LaGuardia as fast as you can," he told the driver, tossing my bag in behind me while I tried to thank him. Between all of this attention and my always noticeable Southern accent, I obviously was not the casual Macy's Christmas shopper.

As we pulled away from the curb, the smiling Asian driver said in his own distinctive accent, "I know who you are!"

"You do?" I replied, somewhat amazed.

"Ah, yes." His smile broadened. "You're one of those *Designing Women!*"

Now it was my turn to smile as I enjoyed a moment of stolen TV stardom.

"Do you enjoy the show?" I asked slyly.

"Yes, indeed. I want to visit the South someday. I want to see the old things." He nodded eagerly.

Speeding along, my new friend and I enthusiastically exchanged stories of our different cultures and how they have changed over the years. I wondered how many people still expect the South to look as it did in the nineteenth century? The South you and I venture through today bears little resemblance to the land the Spaniards and English saw in the early years of the sixteenth century.

Those romantic Spanish explorers who came to Florida must have been real-life Don Quixotes, motivated by dreams of golden streets, emeralds, rubies and pearls the size of kumquats, and, of course, the fountain of youth. They were, after all, men of the medieval world, a Europe ruled by ermine-robed kings and bejeweled men of the church.

The English adventurers, though less flamboyant than the Spaniards, had plans of their own. Like the Spanish, the cavaliers also dreamed of discovering gold and converting the Indians to Christianity. But rather than searching for the fountain of youth, they hoped to find a direct western passage to India. Always concerned with commerce, these practical-minded sixteenth-century English entrepreneurs also planned to send crops and goods back to England from the New World.

In short, the Spaniards were explorers while the Englishmen were settlers.

How different they were. Yet these two very diverse nationalities brought two common loves from their homelands—their festive spirit and their passion for celebration.

If Southerners are a "mythological people" who have created a legendary character about the South and its people, it is because our ancestors brought their myths with them during those days when the world was just emerging from the Dark Ages. The great Greek and Roman conquerors took ancient myths with them to Spain and England in pre-Christian times. Now the Spaniards and English were bringing their own national traditions to the New World.

This is how the Old World traditions of the May Pole, the wassail bowl, Mardi Gras, and the kissing ball came down through history from one country to another, from one generation to another. Our early Southern colonists brought ancient customs as well as their national spirit and character to our shores; they brought their architecture and their gardens; they brought their music and their crafts; they brought their unique styles and their special ways.

What a contrast was this *joie de vivre*, this gaiety, to the somber, self-depriving nature of the purists who settled New England. The Puritans purposefully left their past *behind* and came to the New World to rid themselves of their forefathers' zealous religious traditions. Why, just the names of these different groups

The old-world charm of St. Augustine (above) and New Orleans (opposite) is as real as that of any European village.

of people say so much about them. The New England settlers were Puritans; the Spaniards were conquistadors; the Englishmen were cavaliers.

Throughout the seventeenth century the emigrating Puritans gravitated to the North, where they found others with common beliefs. The South was inhabited by Catholics, Anglicans, and dissenting French Huguenots—infidels, according to the Puritans.

Soon Englishmen who had settled in Barbados, Santo Domingo, and other Caribbean lands began moving to the South, as did the Scotch-Irish. German immigrants settled throughout the southern Piedmont, and at one time there were so many Germans along Louisiana's Mississippi shores that it was called the "German Coast." And who does not remember the story of Evangeline and the French-speaking Acadians of Nova Scotia who, forced out by the British, journeyed down the Mississippi River and became Louisiana's colorful Cajuns?

From halfway around the world, from yet another continent, the blacks brought their rich heritage to the South. Unlike the adventurers who came to seek new fortunes, new lands, and new opportunities, these people came as victims to the Southern shores. They gave much more to their new home than they could reap. Yet they, too, kept alive their customs, traditions, ways, and foods—such important elements of Southern hospitality through the years.

Most important, in their overflowing hearts they brought the woes of humankind and the hope of salvation. Through their songs and folklore we come to know our own sorrows, disappointments, and triumphs of the spirit. This, too, is part of the South that no

other section of the country can claim.

How fortunate we are that our Southern ancestors proudly brought their traditions and cultures with them. In the South they kept their heritage alive. All the while, though, the world was changing rapidly. The medieval period had come to an end and the world was entering a new day—the Period of Enlightenment, the eighteenth century. New traditions and new styles began. As soon as travel and communication between the regions of the

Virginia House, originally built in the sixteenth century, was brought from England and reassembled in Richmond, Virginia, in the 1920s and reflects the South's close ties to its early English heritage.

country became easier and more frequent, many old ways blended together.

Yet we have only to listen to familiar literary voices to realize how distinctly different and strong each one of our country's original cultures was. Fostered by Spanish Florida, we have the high-adventure romances of Ernest Hemingway. Stemming from old English Virginia, we have the idealism of America's Renaissance man, Thomas Jefferson. Originating from strong New England Puritan stock, we have the introspection of Henry David Thoreau. Can you imagine the brooding, dark stories of Herman Melville and Nathaniel Hawthorne coming out of the ebullient South?

Even as we approach the twenty-first century, the character of those early settlers, our ever-festive, convivial, and always romantic Southern ancestors, still dominates the regional character of the South—as does Southern hospitality.

In St. Augustine, Castillo de San Marcos, the impenetrable fort built from coquina shells over three hundred years ago by Spanish soldiers of fortune, stands proud against the lapping waves of the ocean. Only a few blocks away, tiers of Moroccan-red tiles that crown the magnificent nineteenth-century

Ponce de Leon Hotel gleam in the tropical Florida sunlight.

In Virginia, majestic Georgian plantations built in the eighteenth century by Englishmen who aspired to re-create the best of England in the New World dot the winding, heavily wooded, sparsely populated two-lane highway that follows the James River from Richmond to the coast.

History speaks for itself. The deep-rooted cultural differences between the North and South that began in the sixteenth century are neither good nor bad, right nor wrong. They simply exist.

Like the early settlers, today's Southerners have held on to the best of the past by adapting time-tested traditions to modern ways—especially Southern hospitality. We who live in the South think we hold the original patent on the fun, the gaiety, the festivity that makes life rich and full. We believe that good times have never gone out of style. We love sharing all we have with others, and we never miss the opportunity to do so.

That's another way of saying you can travel through Europe and spend thousands of dollars, *or* you can feast your way through the South at a fraction of the cost—and have more fun!

That's why I always chuckle to myself when I run into my friends returning from exhausting European tours. How often they are bedraggled, overextended, and as travel-worn as the luggage they have lost along the way. Their trips to Cannes, Rome, Granada, and Edinburgh sound grand, but so many of the same delights found abroad are right here in the South. No other region in America offers the variety of cultural traditions that have been here since our country was settled.

In Tampa at the Columbia Café in historic Ybor City, whirling skirts and clapping hands moving faster than the eye can behold are as spirited and festive as any you'll see in Seville. Tucked away in Norfolk, Virginia, at the Thoroughgood-Adams House, the wassail dipped from the earthenware bowl on the boldly crafted sixteenth-century English court cupboard is as spicy and rich as that you'll sip in Stratford-on-Avon.

The masked satyrs, pirates, clowns, and devils that dance through the streets night after night during Mardi Gras in Mobile, Alabama, are as colorful and extravagant as those of Rio de Janeiro. And a family-style meal of Southern foods—okra, collard greens, squash, succotash, corn, speckled lima beans, black-eyed peas, tomatoes, fried chicken, catfish, and pork chops, accompanied by corn bread and biscuits, and topped off with pecan pie, pound cake, and rice pudding at Walnut Hill in Vicksburg, Mississippi, is the equal of any European smorgasbord.

A stroll along the quietly rippling lake at Bellingrath Gardens on pathways lined by lush camellia bushes, magnolia trees, and crepe myrtles is as breathtaking as the most perfectly manicured gardens of France. Mysterious, silent columns outside of Windsor, Mississippi, their stories of a different time lost forever, are as haunting as the crumbling ruins of Italy.

The red-coated hunters mounted on chestnut-brown horses that ride to the hounds in the rolling hills of Albemarle County are as colorful as those of the English countryside. And the hospitality dished up in the bed and breakfasts that dot Southern towns of every size, from Eutaw, Alabama, to Houston, Texas, is as warm as that you'll find in any European inn.

And we have so much to offer that can be found only in the South! There are our down-home Texas barbecues, our laid-back North Carolina shag contests, the indescribably beautiful stretches of gently rolling Kentucky bluegrass country, our elegant South Carolina debutante balls, the romance of a warm winter night spent under a full moon on the tropical Key West beaches—to say nothing of the mysterious excitement of a predawn stroll along the narrow, uneven sidewalks of the French Quarter, paths walked long ago by swashbuckling pirates, elegant Creole ladies, and great writers of Southern legends—William Faulkner, Frances Parkinson Keyes, Truman Capote, Ambrose Bierce.

Yes, we Southerners are a myth-loving people and our Southern Elysian Fields are filled with infinite variety. The South's history is rich. Her magic is seductive. Her beauty runs deep. Her irrefutable charm is the hospitality of her people. That's her way.

No wonder people flock to the Natchez Pilgrimage each spring. There, like no place else, time-tested Southern traditions brought from Europe, such as this dance around the maypole, are recreated by each new generation.

~

"Every culture has its southerners . . . who have livelier gestures, more lustrous eyes, more colorful garments, more fancifully decorated vehicles, a wonderful sense of rhythm, and charm, charm, charm. . . ."
Susan Sontag,
The Volcano Lover, A Romance

The Magic of Mardi Gras

*"It seemed as if all the heroes of
antiquity had left their tombs, and their
terrible ghosts were stalking in old majesty
through the streets of Mobile."*
Caldwell Delaney, *Remember Mobile*

Southerners will go to any length to avoid
saying good-bye. We say "Don't stay away
long," "Don't rush off," "See you soon," "I'll
be talking to you," and "You all hurry back"—
for starters. Of course, the best-known parting greeting is one that seems to have been
around forever.

"Ya'll come back!" My New England
father has long delighted in telling how, one
day in 1934, the little Fisher girl who had
just moved to Webster, Massachusetts, from
Lowell, North Carolina, stood on the porch
with her mother, waving good-bye to the
neighborhood children who had come to pay
a proper call. As her new Yankee friends left
she called, in her friendly, deep-Southern
drawl, "Ya'll come back!" They did—leaving
Mrs. Fisher to explain that they should come
back *another* day.

My friend Patrice Baur is hardly a
Southerner. Little matter that she's lived in
Mobile, Alabama, for thirty-plus years. Her
crisp Canadian accent gives her away every
time. But even she has adopted our Southern
ways. That's why, rather than telling me
good-bye after a mid-November visit, she
draped my neck with strands of gold, green,
and purple Mardi Gras beads and said, "See
you at Mardi Gras."

*Green, gold, and
purple, the tradi-
tional Mardi Gras
colors, decorate the
front doors of the
Bragg-Mitchell
House in Mobile,
Alabama, the home
of America's first
Mardi Gras.*

"Now, that's one thing I've always wanted to do," I confessed.

"You must!" Pat exclaimed. "You're not
a *true* Southerner until you've been to Mardi
Gras! Anyway, you have to have Mardi Gras
in *Southern Hospitality*."

"I plan to," I agreed, for New Orleans'
famed Mardi Gras definitely was on my list of
must-get-to celebrations. But then I showed
my ignorance.

"Do you know what day Mardi Gras
comes on next year?" I asked, digging in my
pocketbook for my calendar. Worse yet, I
tagged on, "I think it would be wonderful to
get to New Orleans for the festivities."

That's when I learned that Mardi Gras is
not a day-long celebration, but a free-wheel-
ing two-week, sometimes two-month, affair,
and that Mobile, *not* New Orleans, is the
home of America's first Mardi Gras.

Have you guessed? Yes, four months later, decked out in gold, green, and purple beads
and doused with confetti, Walter and I were
two of the most exuberant frolickers in Mobile—dancing, parading, and carousing away
four memorable nights.

Historians and folklorists tell us that
Mardi Gras has its origins in such pagan celebrations as Bacchanalia, Lupercalia, and Sat-
urnalia—festivities that became Christianized
and spread from Europe through the entire
western hemisphere with the French and
Spanish explorers. Along the way the raucous
carnival became an amalgamation of many
cultures and ways. Elements from Caribbean,
African as well as Afro-American, Latin, Creole, even Anglican celebrations were added
to the Mardi Gras traditions originally
brought from France and Spain.

Today native Mobilians gleefully tell you

that our American Mardi Gras began *in Mobile* on New Year's Eve in 1832 when a party of intoxicated young men created bedlam by parading along the streets, ringing in the New Year with cowbells they had "borrowed" from the town's hardware store. That's how the Cowbellian de Rakin Society was born.

Somehow and at some uncertain time, their antics got pushed ahead to Twelfth Night. (After all, New Year's Eve is cause enough to celebrate.) That way those bawdy young men had an excuse for frolicking from January 6 all the way through Shrove Tuesday, the day before the fasting Lenten season began. (What a contrast that fun, weeks-long merriment is to the traditional Shrove Tuesday pancake dinner at the church parlor held in most parts of the United States!)

Like so many Southern traditions, Mardi Gras was interrupted by the Civil War. But only temporarily. In 1866 Joe Cain, dressed like an Indian, paraded through the city streets in a charcoal wagon, creating good humor and much-needed laughter to war-weary, defeated Mobile. The irrepressible spirit of Mardi Gras was back. When the Order of Myths (the Double O Ms) paraded through the town in 1868, Mobile's grand Mardi Gras festivities began in earnest.

To the rest of the world these origins are mostly long-forgotten memories. Few people outside of Mobile know about the city's mystic societies,—the Strikers, Mystics of Time, the Knights of Revelry, and the OOM's (to name a few)—that keep the tradition and myths of Joe Cain, Felix, and Folly and Death alive. You don't have to know the history to enjoy the festivities.

If I could have my way, every door in America would be decked out in bright, exuberant Mardi Gras decorations, which are as cheerful and spirit-lifting as any Christmas wreath.

The fun of it all is why more and more Northern tourists are flocking to New Orleans and Mobile these days to capture the festive, carefree spirit of "the season." In fact, each year totally frivolous Mardi Gras celebrations are spreading a wee bit farther north—not just to Virginia and Maryland, but to New York and Boston. Always remember, though, it is the rich traditions and their uniquely Southern origins that make Mardi Gras the *most* Southern of all celebrations.

Once you've been to a Mardi Gras, you know why visitors are attracted from all over. The night of our first Mardi Gras parade in Mobile was unforgettably magical.

Though the parties, dances, parades, and celebrations had been going on for weeks, the best and the biggest always fall on the last three or four days before Ash Wednesday.

Don't even try to do anything but have fun. The whole city is on a long holiday. It truly is party time!

We arrived on Saturday, February 21, for four devil-may-care days before Ash Wednesday. It was a warm early-spring day in this jewel of the deep South. But a brisk sea breeze blew ashore by twilight—the time when thousands of merrymakers from every direction spewed out of homes and hotels, cars and buses, into the streets. The weather was the last thing on anyone's mind.

Fun-loving, rebel-rousing spectators pressed three and four deep against the guard rails lining the parade route. Mink-jacketed ladies and gentlemen in white tie and tails on their way to formal balls and cocktail parties stood next to groups of bar-hopping, T-shirted, blue-jeaned college kids

Beads and bows for little girls, masks and grand balls for adults, parades for frolickers and revelers of every age. Once you've fallen under the charm of Mardi Gras, it never leaves you.

who never even felt the chilly nighttime air.

Children of every description, knowing they could stay up past their bedtime, wriggled their way to the front to peer through adult legs.

The convivial scene reminded me of a huge block party. There wasn't a stranger in the crowd. "Hey, Joe! Margaret! Over here! What are you doing here?" You'd have thought nearby neighbors were long-lost friends the way they yelled out when they caught a glimpse of one another through the crowd and across the way.

"Where are you from?" "Did you say you're from Georgia?" "I'm from western Arkansas. Have you ever been there?" Total strangers gabbed as if they were cousins, or at least kissin' kin. It took only a casual greeting for visitors from other towns and distant states to become instant buddies.

Conversations flowed as free and easy as the rainbow-colored confetti that rained down from the lacy balconies of the old brick downtown buildings where the native Mobilians traditionally take their perch. Noisy vendors pushing wildly decorated carts bellowed out their wares. The streets hummed in a carnival mood that reached a grand crescendo when distant trumpet blares and pulsing, deep, booming drums suddenly sliced through the damp night air.

Little children tugged at the closest available sleeve, begging "Pick me up!" Loving couples snuggled close. A jubilant cheer erupted from the crowd as the first mounted police heralded the start of the parade.

What a spectacularly noisy, exciting scene it was! The horses danced from side to side, their hooves clopping out their own rhythm against the pavement. High-spirited

Mardi Gras is a suspended world of grown-up make-believe. For just a few hours of your life, when you don a costume, you can become anyone you wish to be. That is a pleasure everyone should experience at least once. I think I'll go back some day. Only this time I'm going to buy a mask—and wear it!

To reign at a Mardi Gras ball, if only for just a few hours, is a magical experience.

and high-stepping majorettes, their fringed white and gold skirts whipping about like the horses' manes, strutted to the jazzy, rapping beat of the drums. Brightly costumed maskers bunched close together, their long arms loaded up to their shoulders with shiny, wonderfully gaudy Mardi Gras beads, made a colorful sight as they half marched, half skipped to the blaring bursts of the brass trumpets and tubas.

"Here! Here!" the crowd shouted. They had come not just for the parade, but for the beads, the copper- and silver-colored doubloons, and most of all, the chocolate-covered, cream-filled, melt-in-your-mouth Moon Pies—the gotta-get booty the children and adults alike hustled to gather up and hoard like precious pirate's treasure.

When Walter scrambled to catch a fake pearl necklace flying through the air, snared it, and playfully tossed it around my neck, I caught the fever.

"Free jewels! Look! They must be ten millimeters! Now, that's real Southern hospitality!" I squealed, full of abandon, laughing all the way. For when you catch the fever, you know that Mardi Gras is reason enough to laugh, to revel, to cast your worries aside, to forget yesterday's and tomorrow's cares, and to celebrate today.

On and on they came. A mile-long parade of band after band, float after float, rounded the bend. Huge papier-mâché figures of every description bobbed up and down on bigger-than-life floats. Glistening under thousands of bright-white lights, fire-eating dragons, fierce sea serpents, exotic birds, grotesque heads, fanciful spirits, and mythological heroes wound and twisted along the very same streets where the Cowbellians strutted and made merry over a century and a half earlier.

That same impetuous rebel spirit still lives, but the rowdies no longer walk the streets. Modern-day "Cowbellians" ride atop their society's floats. Who cares that the float tosses and jolts with every stop and sudden lurch? For one night each year those doctors and lawyers, accountants and businessmen wantonly sway with every bounce and bobble of the bumpy trip. This is their proudest hour.

For a full year they have dreamed and designed, worked and played, to make this glorious moment a reality. Disguised in every conceivable garb—as clowns, swashbuckling buccaneers, French courtiers, Spanish conquistadors—they toss *more* candy, *more* necklaces, *more* trinkets and favors, *more* Moon Pies, out of bottomless bags into the expectant crowd.

That night, like every other night of Mardi Gras the crowd cheered louder and louder as their eyes drank in the spectacle and their eager hands raked in their prizes.

Painted in brilliant silver and gold, reds and pinks, yellows and blues, each float is seemingly more fantastic than the one just before. The bands try to outplay one another. And each row of horses that rides by prances more playfully, trots more majestically.

For just a few minutes, time stood still that night. A never-ending array of sparkling beads, fanciful sights, trinkets and spangles, miles of curly-cue paper streamers, colors, lights, music, strutters and maskers thrilled our senses and kept us poised for the next magical surprise until, too soon, the final float lumbered out of view, its fringed skirt flapping in the breeze. The crowd disappeared as quickly as it had gathered. But the night, and its merriment, had only begun. Parties and dances awaited.

Months of preparations go into making each one of the many black- or white-tie balls held every year even more beautiful, more spectacular, more exquisite, more memorable than all of those that have gone before. No detail, or expense, it would appear, is spared. Hotels, clubs, banquet halls, civic and convention buildings, private and public meeting places all have been booked for months, sometimes years, in advance.

There will be the customary dancing, of course, but first comes the traditional tableau.

For those of you unfamiliar with these vignettes, imagine this spellbinding moment, all the while pretending that you are in antebellum Mobile, let's say in 1858, a time long before radio, movies, and TV.

The room becomes dark. Silence falls. On stage, heavy folds of velvet curtains roll back. There, silhouetted against a bigger-than-life backdrop, a scene appears. The room is transformed into a frozen, magical moment. Before your enraptured eyes is a scene so magnificent it could have been lifted straight from an opulent grand opera, or be a stolen glimpse into an elegant eighteenth-century European masked ball. Motionless figures are resplendent in lace, velvet, and shimmering lamé costumes made more breathtaking and dazzling by the thousands of tiny rhinestones, pearls, and spangles that catch the light like the fanciful ever-elusive patterns of a whirling kaleidoscope.

In those days the tableaux depictions mostly came from history, a novel or legend, or everyone's favorite—mythology. The captivated audience thrilled to splendid scenes of Neptune surrounded by sea nymphs and dolphins, or a romantic view of ever-cunning Cupid with his bow and arrows, watching

over Venus and Psyche at their wedding feast, their flower-bedecked bodies entwined, momentarily immortalized in a loving embrace.

On this Mardi Gras night in 1993, we were equally dazzled by a breathtaking re-creation of a mist-enshrouded underground scene from the current musical *Phantom of the Opera*. Today, like yesterday, the subject is only a vehicle for the splendor.

The tableau lasted only a few seconds, then through the stillness, a huge puff of smoke followed by a cloud of balloons exploded. The curtain dropped, signaling that it was time for the evening's festivities to begin.

Watching, enthralled, as the scene came to an end and the room rocked with applause, I recalled a description of a Mobile tableau that I had found in an old book, *Mr. Christopher Katydid*, a long-forgotten 1864 English novel. "*As the curtain fell over each tableau, there were murmurs of applause and exclamations of delight from the vast assemblage; and when the last tableau, representing Aurora, was duly represented, the throng of gods, obeying the signal warble of Mars' whistle, formed a line and*

After their formal introduction, the royal court awaits the beginning of yet another night of high-spirited celebration until the wee hours of the morning.

Fine silver, crystal, and linen adorn Her Majesty, Queen Tullulah's table (right).

Walter and I adorned with our beads, doubloons, twisted white tie and all, as we celebrate a never-to-be-forgotten night (above)!

Of all the beautiful wonders I beheld that memorable Mardi Gras, the black velvet train worn by Queen Shannon (opposite) emblazoned in thousands of twinkling red, green, gold, and silver lights, was as magnicifent as any.

slowly marched around the parquet to one of the weird and solemn marches of Mendelssohn."

How the ceremony, the magic, and the mystery of the tableaux remain timeless through the years! These enchanting tableaux are a bit of yesteryear fantasy kept alive only in the deep South. They should not be missed.

Much to my surprise, I am now an expert on Mardi Gras balls—and each one is different. At some, the final tableau is followed by supper, or the dance officially begins. At others the presentation of debutantes (appropriately designated as the queen and her court) comes next. In any case, the night is never long enough, and dawn definitely comes too early during the last days of Mardi Gras.

Each night I, too, danced into the wee hours. What woman, dressed in her loveliest ballgown and enraptured by the glamour of

the moment, wants to keep Cinderella hours—especially when there are so many other beautiful dresses and jewels to see and, in our case, so many interesting new friends to meet? Even the youngest children brought by their parents to see an older cousin, or sister, or neighbor's son in the court stayed far into the night. In short, Mardi Gras revelers and maskers know no curfews, at any age.

Yet dawn invariably comes, and with it a day chock full of more festivities. Most mornings the first parade begins by eleven. There are so many activities to work in during the season that several get bunched up at the end. There's the Order of Polka Dots Parade, the Pharoah's Parade, the Floral Parade, King Elexis's Arrival, the Joe Cain Parade, King Felix's Arrival, the Comic Cowboys Parade, the King and Knights' Parade—it goes on and on. But that just gives everyone even more to do, all the more to see.

These daytime parades have a character distinctly different from the moonlight ones. But never fear. Mardi Gras' grandeur and festivity hardly fades with the daybreak. The brilliant Southern sun paints the floats a hot red and white. The silver tinsel almost blinds you at midday. And the crowd loves it all.

All day long people leisurely saunter up and down the streets, wandering out of the coffeeshops, lunchrooms, stores, and hotels that line the downtown parade routes. And if the ongoing parades themselves are not fantastic enough, you never know what strange sights you'll see around every corner.

During Mardi Gras, Mobile's streets are a mass of ever-changing colors, intoxicating musical rhythms, and irresistible aromas of once-a-year carnival food.

A red devil scoots by, then shimmies

across the street. A bony skeleton rattles along eating cotton candy. Over there a purple-haired and lavender-stockinged lady flirts from beneath her ruffle-fringed green and gold umbrella. And coming around the bend is a star-spangled Uncle Sam.

At noon on the last day of Mardi Gras, half dancing, half strutting to the bands (by now I had really dived right in!), I broke into gales of laughter as I watched a group of exuberant young band musicians high-step around a group of slightly overwhelmed, slow-moving, late-middle-age tourists. The kids had reached the end of their parade route and now, arms linked to form a human caterpillar, they were retracing their steps through the streets. Their teenage spirits were sky high, and their laughter was contagious.

As they wove around our twosome, I felt their electricity. Like those who had brought Mardi Gras to this land so long ago, here were blacks and whites of Caribbean, African, European, English, and Latin origins—boys and girls—frolicking and celebrating together. Here was a unique Southern tradition alive and well—a tradition that once sprang from many cultures but today is just *Southern.* Passing before us was the South of yesterday and the South of tomorrow.

One small fellow near the end of the line was having a heck of a time keeping up with the other taller, larger kids. Coming up on our group, he had to straddle the curb to keep his balance and at the same time keep from sweeping me out into the street. As he wobbled by he called out, "Excuse me, ma'am."

"Your mom taught you some good manners," Walter called back in his jovial voice.

I laughed up at him. "Yep, a little Southern hospitality, Mardi Gras style!"

A Riotous King Cake

~

It was one of those steamy late-June afternoons. Walter and I were sitting around the Formica-top table at the Magnolia Grill in St. Francisville, Louisiana.

While waiting for our orders he picked up a copy of the local free newspaper—the type every town has these days. "Listen to this," he laughed.

This letter-to-the-editor was so enjoyable that I must share excerpts from it with you. Local customs *are* baffling—even to someone from another area of the South.

Dear Friends,

A couple of weeks ago three of us traveled through your area. We stopped at a delightful cabin that was serving as a welcome center and museum. I cannot remember the name of the place, but the lady was so friendly and answered our multitude of questions.

However, [another] question. On page 21 you had a recipe for King Cake for Mardi Gras. I want to try this one—but one place in the recipe directions the directions are "place the baby anywhere in the filling." I guess I am dense, or just don't understand Mardi Gras and its customs. Could you help an ignorant "hillbilly" from Tennessee?

Respectfully, Marie East

Quickly admitting that we cannot take for granted things that *we* know, Dorcas Brown, the publisher, eagerly cleared up Marie's and, I'm sure, many other people's puzzlement.

South Louisianians know that the baby is a small plastic figure placed in the King Cake, and the person who gets it in their piece must host the party. But if you didn't know that, the directions certainly would have sounded strange, to say the least. Now the Mardi Gras custom of King Cakes can move safely into Tennessee with no harm to young children. Thanks for writing, Marie.

COUNTRY ROADS' KING CAKE

~

Makes two 1-pound King Cakes

For your Mardi Gras party, anywhere, here is Country Roads' King Cake recipe, which, Dorcas says, "Anyone who has made bread (or those who have not) can make."

½ cup plus 2 tablespoons sugar, divided
2 ¼-ounce packets dry yeast
⅓ cup warm water
1 stick (8 tablespoons) margarine
⅔ cup evaporated milk
2 teaspoons salt
4 medium eggs
6 cups all-purpose flour

1. Combine the 2 tablespoons sugar, yeast, and water in a large bowl. Let the mixture stand until it foams.

2. Place the margarine, milk, ½ cup sugar, and salt in a small saucepan and melt it slowly.

3. Beat the eggs into the foaming yeast. When the milk mixture is lukewarm, add it to the eggs.

4. Add the flour a little at a time. Knead the dough for 5 to 10 minutes.

5. Grease another large bowl with additional margarine. Place the dough in the bowl, turn

"They had no pleasure so great as taking care of other people."
Letitia M. Burwell, Elkwood, Virginia, 1861

the dough, and then cover the bowl with a wet cloth. Let the dough rise until doubled, about 2 hours in a warm place, then begin the filling process and ice. (Directions follow.)

6. Cover and set the filled dough in a warm place to rise until it has doubled in bulk. This may take as long as 3 hours. Meanwhile, preheat the oven to 350° F.

7. Bake the cake for 18 to 20 minutes, or until golden brown. (A cake without filling will take about 15 minutes.) Test for doneness. A filled cake will flatten out when baked. An unfilled cake will be puffy. Allow the cake to cool before icing.

FILLINGS
Cream-cheese type: Mix together a package of cooked vanilla pudding and an 8-ounce package of cream cheese.
Fruit filling: Use canned pie fillings.
Any tasty commerical dessert, cake, or pastry filling or even exceptionally good preserves can be used.
Baby (for good luck)

1. Divide the dough into 2 pieces. Roll out 1 piece of dough to about 18 inches long and 6 inches wide to make one small cake.

2. Spread your choice of filling lengthwise down the center. Avoid overfilling. The sides should close easily once the filling is in. The dough should not be stretched and weakened.

3. Place the baby anywhere in the filling.

4. Fold the dough in half and pinch the two long edges together. Turn the cake so that the seam is on the bottom. Bring the two ends together to make a circle. Tuck one end inside the other, then tuck the exposed edges for a neat connection.

ICING
¼ cup (½ stick) margarine
1 pound box confectioners' sugar
¼ teaspoon salt
½ cup simple syrup (¼ cup sugar and ¼ cup water, heated until sugar is dissolved)

FOR DECORATING
Colored sugar
Sliced almonds
Candied cherries

1. Blend together the margarine, confectioners' sugar, salt, and simple syrup. Spread it on the cake.

2. Decorate with flowers made of sliced almonds and candied cherries, then sprinkle colored sugar (made by mixing 3 or 4 drops of food coloring into granulated sugar) over the icing.

Who would imagine that baked inside this scrumptuous pastry is a "plastic baby"? The King's Cake tradition began in the twelfth century as a cake made for Epiphany or Twelfth Night. In the early cakes, whoever found a bean, crown, or coin in his slice was declared "King for the Day." Now the lucky person who finds the baby is expected to host next year's King Cake party.

In darkness worshipers gather on Easter in Old Salem...

No matter how exciting the adventures, how rich the discoveries, how warm and welcoming the people, or how much fun you are having, everyone needs a rest. So Walter gets the blame for this leg of our journey—a blame he rightfully boasts about.

We set out from Washington on Maundy Thursday of Easter Week because Walter's longtime friend, Fred Crouch, a Winston-Salem, North Carolina, native, simply kept telling him in persuasive terms, "You *have* to go to Old Salem for the Moravian sunrise service." I admit that a certain degree of personal guilt made it easy for Walter to win me over. Most of my fifty-three years have been spent within a hundred miles of Winston-Salem. I cannot count the number of times I have wandered the historic and enchanting streets of the quaint village. But I had never been there for the town's most famous event, the Moravian Easter morning service.

Easter Sunday Love Feast

~

I really hadn't planned to go anywhere for Easter. After all, Walter and I had been on the road continually for two and a half months.

There are no fancy bonnets, frills, or bows, nor any of the latest fashions in the predawn Easter parade that winds its way along the century-old cobblestone walkways in Old Salem, the little Moravian village tucked inside the town of Winston-Salem. But there is a brass band whose sweet hymns echo through the primeval trees to welcome the rising sun and happy morning.

There are no pink and yellow Easter baskets filled to the brim with colorfully dyed eggs and long-eared chocolate candy bunnies. But there are still-warm, plump hot cross buns like those that peasants sold but kings ate.

There are no merry revelers on Easter Sunday morning in this quiet corner of piedmont North Carolina. But everyone is welcomed, and the commemoration casts a uplifting spell that is as powerful in its own way as the jubilant magic of Mardi Gras eight hundred miles farther south.

The spell begins when the dark, heavy cloud of night is lifted by dawn's soft colors and the morning sun spreads light upon the earth and the throngs of devout worshipers. It is a wondrous scene—a time of untold beauty and joy, hopefulness and thanksgiving. It is a time of rich, loving hospitality—the sort that comes when a deep, personal experience is shared with other people.

Like so many other Southern celebrations of hospitality, this one, too, began in Europe, but quickly found its way to colonial America. In 1732 in Herrnhut, Germany, a group of young Moravian men originated the idea of holding an Easter service in a graveyard where they could celebrate Christ's symbolic rising and greet the morning with hymns of praise. Old Salem's traditional service has been held every year since 1772.

Last Easter, like each year, in the darkest hour of the night before the dawn, while the moon was still high in the cloudless sky, thousands of visitors of every sect, creed, and race flocked to the streets of Old Salem. Theirs were the faces of the faithful, the devoted. Generations of families passed by. Grandmothers held tight to chubby little fingers. Young marrieds and even teenagers were everywhere in sight. It was a chilly morning, and I smiled at the sight of sleeping babies, snuggled against their parents' warm down jackets. And there were the braver souls—families dressed for later church services in lighter noonday attire.

As the hushed crowd rustled along the uneven sidewalks and darkened streets, one by one the lights in the old brick and timber houses came on. Soon the entire sleeping

town was awakened to a rousing chorus of "Sleepers, Wake!" played by scores of Moravian musicians. Silently, visitors and residents alike hurried to the steps of the Home Church. When the many thousands were gathered, the minister appeared and loudly proclaimed, "The Lord is risen!"

"The Lord is risen indeed!" the congregation resounded in unison, as they have for

...to greet the morning sun with songs of praise and hopes for peace.

Hot cross buns (top) and gingerbread are Easter favorites in Old Salem.

almost two and a quarter centuries. Then together as one body, the band—playing as they proceeded—the crowd, and the church leaders walked the well-worn path to God's Acre (as Moravian cemeteries are called). There, within its walled sanctity, among the perfectly lined, freshly scrubbed squares that mark the resting places where the Moravian brothers and sisters have "fallen asleep in the Lord," prayers were given, hymns were sung, and antiphonal brass choruses were played as we awaited the dawning of Easter morn.

To our backs the bright moon that had lighted our way slowly began to lose its glow as the sky turned from pitch black to an azure blue. Silently and wondrously a soft yellow-pink glow spread over us. Then in a sudden burst from behind the majestic, newly leafed trees in the east, the sun appeared.

Even at that emotionally charged moment there was no fanfare. "Go forth," the

benediction was pronounced. In the distance the last deep, compelling tones of the brass horns hung in the morning mist, bringing, for another year, the sacred service to an end. Yet few of the worshipers left. Peacefully, reverently, the guests strolled through the resting field where all people are equal.

We lingered behind, enjoying the morning air and the sights all around us. While Walter took a few last pictures, I began reading, one by one, the inscriptions on the markers. Like the Easter morning service, their poignant messages were simple, yet so eloquent. I paused and read aloud: "May the Lord Watch Between me and thee / While we are absent One from the Other."

By now the fully risen sun shone in its full Southern glory. The dewdrops on the fresh spring flowers that marked each grave sparkled like bright diamonds. "Walter," I said, "I'm awfully glad you made me come."

The serene hospitality of historic Old Salem is never more beautiful than in the early morning spring light (left).

Easter would not be Easter without its newly blossoming flowers. These picture-perfect tulips on the steps of an Old Salem home are a cheery invitation to enter.

I hope you will love the old plantation for the sake of the happy children who lived there.
ELLEN MORDECAI IN HER NINETY-THIRD YEAR, 1912

I Dreamt That I Dwelt

Bathed in shadows, wrapped in ribbons of sunlight, framed by an allée of stately oaks or magnolias, Southern homes are hauntingly beautiful, eternally romantic. Their welcoming doors fling open to rooms furnished with a family's things—splendid walnut and rich, yellow pine furnishings, treasured, mellow heirloom silver, fragile, handpainted antique china lovingly passed down from one generation to another. Here the picturesque comes to life. ⁓ Every room holds cherished memories. What tales of gentle laughter and raucous gaiety, splendid parties and simple gatherings those walls could tell!

In St. Francisville, Louisiana, stands elegant Rosedown (above). The huge bed in the "best chamber" (below) was made for Henry Clay to take to the White House. When he lost the election, the bed came to Rosedown instead.

them these dwellings hold history, mystery, and a dream of a longed-for Southern lifestyle.

As long ago as 1774, when Philip Fithian of New Jersey saw Nomini, a grand eighteenth-century Virginia plantation, he said, "The House appears most romantic, at the same time that it does truly elegant." Those words ring as true of so many Southern homes today as they did then. That's why these remarkable homes and their contents are the embodiment of Southern hospitality to all who come to see them.

At Rosedown I could hardly keep myself from slipping away to climb up the bedsteps and tumble onto the majestic, canopied four-poster bedstead in the "best chamber." And I always wanted to peek into the corner cupboards and into the bottom cabinets of the walnut huntboards to see what treasures might be there.

But since I can't, I love old books about historic homes. Some passages were wonderful in their simplicity. "The old homestead was quite antique in appearance. Inside, the high mantelpieces reaching nearly to the ceiling, which was also high, and the high wainscoting, together with the old furniture, made a picture of the olden time," wrote Letitia Burwell in 1860, describing a colonial Virginia home.

Even in unpretentious homes the surroundings could make visits more hospitable, as discovered Frederick Law Olmsted, who traveled through the South as a young journalist long before he made his fame as a landscape architect. "We were seated in rocking-chairs in a well-furnished room, before a blazing fire, offered water to wash, in a little lean-to bed-room, and though we had two hours to wait for our supper, it was most

Each piece holds a special story. A brass-bound leather box can open a flood of smiles or tears. A china teapot can transport you back to a warm kitchen and the delicious aroma of cinnamon tea on a cold day.

Southerners have always loved such nostalgia, such sentiment. And so do the millions of tourists from other parts of the country who stream to the South to see the plantation homes of another time and another place. To

Inviting nooks in Rosedown's music room (top) and bedrooms. This special cupboard (left) alongside the fireplace is for warming guests' night clothes.

*These breathtakingly
beautiful rooms are
not scenes from
museum homes.
They are venues of
Southern homes lived
in by families—many
of which can trace
their ancestry back
to the people who
gathered the heir-
loom furnishings
and decorations from
near-to-home and
around the world.
In the South, history,
heritage, and beauty
are part of our
daily lives.*

In the presence of mementos of a bygone era—a gleaming mahogany chest, its drawers lined in picturesque wallpaper (right), a grandmother's sterling silver brushes and crocheted dresser scarf—time seems to stand still as we long for a more leisurely life when families gathered for long visits, grand celebrations, and, of course, Southern hospitality.

excellent, and we passed an agreeable evening in intelligent conversation with our host," he wrote from Texas in the winter of 1856.

Other descriptions were exotic and evocative, like this memory of Point Saint Pierre, a home that once stood on Edisto Island, South Carolina. "I see before me that grand old colonial house, with its twelve great rooms, with white and colored marble for its inside adornment; the spiral 'flying stair'; its brown stone front steps; its double piazzas . . . with its extensive grounds of ornamental shrubs and imported cedars . . . all enclosed with moss-covered live oaks, on a point where two rivers meet on their journey to the sea three miles away, with not a tree to obstruct the view."

Yet other passages capture the opulence of the antebellum deep South, where splendor reigned. This is a picture of the Louisiana plantation Nottoway, as described by Harnett Kane. "Then there was the ultimate in plantation splash—doorknobs of porcelain, each hand-painted in a different design of roses, lilies, or magnolias, with matching keyhole covers. About the house [there were] two hundred windows, twelve mantels of Italian Carrara or black Austrian marble, five stairways in addition to the main one, bronze chandeliers shaped into the heads of grinning pagan gods, and a row of fifteen slave bells—each in a different tone to summon the domestics to the proper rooms."

And the furnishings themselves evoked such lovely descriptions. "The furniture was old-timey," wrote Thomas Nelson Page in *The Old South*. "Mahogany and rosewood bedsteads and dressers black with age, and polished till they shone like mirrors, hung with draperies white as snow; straight-backed

chairs generations old interspersed with common new ones; long sofas; old shining tables with slender, brass-tipped legs, straight or fluted, holding some fine old books, and in springtime a blue or flowered bowl or two with glorious roses; bookcases filled with brown-backed, much-read books."

The beauty of Southern homes is timeless. These dwellings glow with a warmth that comes from loving and appreciating the very best life has to offer—books, flowers, well-crafted objects, fine food.

Lovely surroundings and beautiful things truly add an air of graciousness to family life. They are the material embodiment of Southern hospitality. There is nothing more appealing or deeply comforting than the security of home. Our hearts long for it. No wonder we cherish our beautiful Southern homes and family things so much.

～

"The home remains lovely
after the guests are gone."
Archibald Rutledge, *Home by the River*.

At The Elms in Natchez, I remembered these words written in 1899, "When I saw the beautiful Southern home, with its flowers and bowers and sunshine, I said to myself, 'Now they will see how we live, and will envy us.'"

Along I-95, highway signs beckon you toward Route 5, where the lasting, often disarming charm of Sherwood Forest (above and opposite) and other plantation homes awaits.

The day we visited, Wink, the family dog, was lounging in the historic ballroom (opposite, top) that is still used for family celebrations, as is the dining room (opposite, bottom).

Gentle-Born Families, Princely Hospitality

"On the 9th of April 1835 I left Richmond, and embarked on the James river, the banks of which received the first settlers that Britain sent across the Atlantic," the Honorable Charles Augustus Murray wrote home to England when he was twenty-nine years old.

"The morning was fine, and the view of the receding city extremely beautiful. The banks of the river are generally well wooded and cultivated, and every now and then is seen a country-house more resembling those in England than any which I had hitherto observed. . . . In Virginia as in England, a country-house is a very hothouse of acquain-

tance, and ripens it much earlier than the common garden of society; and the hospitality of Virginia is deservedly celebrated."

Over 150 years later, the James River plantations remain much as they were, not just in 1835, but in 1785, some even in 1735 and earlier. The names of those who built those homes—the Carters, the Randolphs, the Tylers, and the Harrisons—are not just names on ivy-covered headstones or leather-bound books laid out for tourists to see. The Carters, the Randolphs, the Tylers, and the Harrisons are the names of the people who take you through these stately homes, who chat with you on the wide lawns that roll down to the James, and who greet you at the convenience stores scattered along Virginia Route 5.

Though it is close to thriving, ever-changing Norfolk and Richmond, the plantation region of Tidewater Virginia and its woods and farmland that stretch along the James River from Chesapeake Bay to Richmond, remain little changed.

It is beautiful land, green through the long summer, gold and purple in the fall, brown and gray during the short-lived winter, and pink and yellow in the glorious springtime. An ivy tree shades a kudzo-shrouded barn. A cornfield stretches beneath a cloudless sky. A shadowy allée of oaks canopies a red dirt path. Peaceful, pleasing sights roll over you. And the houses!

The elegant, refined houses the wealthy landowners built on this picturesque land face the calm, wide James River that brought them not just provisions, but news and visitors. It was, and is, a perfect blending of land and water, earth and sky.

Inside, the homes are spacious but not

showy. Deep wainscoting and molding creates a feeling of grandness, not grandeur.

That is why, to my way of thinking, nowhere can you capture an immediate sense of our colonial past as poignantly as you can in the James River plantations that have stood so proudly and so well through the centuries. Nowhere can you bask in a moment out of the past, frozen in time, the way you can when you step over the threshold into a family's dwelling—such as Shirley or Sherwood Forest—homes still lived in by descendants of the legendary Carter and Tyler families.

It is thrilling to be in a room that is decorated with actual objects from the period, still in place the way they were intended to be—heirloom silver on the sideboard, family portraits in the living room, an eighteenth-century candlestick on the bedside table, a rustic kettle by the fireplace. And there are the wonderful stories associated with the homes and the objects.

There's a sterling silver bowl at Shirley, the Carters' home, engraved "Nestor," the name of a champion horse. It is told that after a big win, Nestor would drink his victory champagne from that bowl. Why not?

And you almost feel like you're eavesdropping when you hear that Julia Gardiner Tyler used to complain that the railing on the back porch at Sherwood Forest needed constant whitewashing because her husband, President John Tyler, would put his feet up on it. These stories make history live and houses homes. They make the aristocracy just plain folks.

The lure of James River plantations is their past—their age, their history, but most of all their association with the people of another time, a bygone era. Who can think of

To save Wilton (above and opposite, top) from impending destruction in the 1930s, the Colonial Dames of Virginia moved the Randolphs' home-place to nearby Richmond. In the 18th century, the spacious hallway was used for dances!

The next time you're in a wonderful historic home, let your imagination flow. Suddenly a family's dwelling, as well as their "things," will take on an air of romance and excitement.

That's what Kay Montgomery did when planning her wedding at Sherwood Forest to William Tyler, President Tyler's great-grandson. In 1845 Tyler had commissioned a wing built onto Sherwood Forest—a long narrow room, sixty-eight feet by twelve feet, which was ideal for the popular Virginia reel. It still is. When Kay and William were married there in May 1993, a fiddler and caller and the wedding guests did what Tylers and their friends have done for generations: They danced the Virginia reel. There was at least one difference though. Kay and William's wedding was the usual noonday affair. In the 1850 era the ball began at 8 P.M. and the first breakfast (turkey, venison, and ham with the fat one inch thick) was served at 1:30, followed by a second dessert breakfast at 3:30 A.M. (ice cream, wine jelly, German fortune cookies, cake, and whole cream flavored with wine).

Kay herself told me those stories. She was taking tours through the house the day we were there. And Danish-born Helle Carter told me about Nestor's silver bowl. Her husband, Hill, is the tenth-generation direct descendant of the family that built Shirley in the seventeenth century.

Take a trip along the James River and you'll know why, in 1833, Henry Barnard of Connecticut, after visiting Shirley Plantation, wrote to his sister back North, "My Dear Betty, I think you would delight to visit this region . . . and to experience the princely hospitality of the *gentle* born families."

It is still so today.

people without remembering their homes and the objects they loved? A sense of place anchors us in life. Why, Scarlett wouldn't be Scarlett without Tara.

Have you ever allowed your mind to wander when listening as the guide tells you that three or four, or more, presidents dined in the very room you're standing in? They did at Berkeley and Wilton. Can't you see Jefferson, wineglass in hand, pondering the fate of the nation, extolling the worth of the farmer, or, better yet, telling about his own latest shipment of French wines?

The restored kitchen at Shirley (above), the Hills' and Carters' home for eleven generations. In the drawing room at Berkeley (left) we are in awe of the history associated with this 1726 home of William Henry Harrison, our ninth president.

Natchez

WHERE THE OLD SOUTH STILL LIVES

"This is the country for me."
Samuel Grier, May 1843

〜

"Haven't been to Natchez?" my Raleigh friend, Martha Beahm, exclaimed incredulously, even reprimandingly. *"You,* of all people. Well, you must!"

Dear reader, if *you* haven't been to Natchez, well, you must!

It's embarrassing for a writer to fall back on clichés like "nostalgic journey," "beautiful beyond description," "ghosts from the past," "antebellum splendor," and that hackneyed, travelogue phrase you hear repeatedly in Natchez, "where the Old South still lives." But when you're writing about Natchez you know that everything that could be said about this enchanting gem of a town "where the Old South still lives" already has been—over and over. Everyone who visits this tucked-away hamlet built on Mississippi River dreams falls under her tantalizing spell.

Of course, there's always the danger of being disappointed when you've heard so much about a place. So I took along my cavalier I'm-from-Virginia spirit the first time I went to Natchez. Show me, I challenged her. She did.

She showed me remarkable homes—both magnificent and charming—exquisite gardens, and breathtaking landscapes. She shared with me soul-stirring legends that made me

High above the mighty Mississippi, Natchez is a charmed place...

weep. Best of all, she welcomed me and showered me with courtesy and hospitality. This is not to say that everything in Natchez is perfect.

One year when I was there on December 23, streams of sweat, not perspiration, trickled down between my shoulder blades. It was over 80 degrees and the humidity was 100 percent. Another time I had to lug "Attila the Hun," as I fondly call my closet-on-wheels suitcase, up two steep flights of twisting, narrow, high-pitched back porch steps to get to my room. (I sweated then, too.) And don't even try to find a late-night snack, to say nothing of a quiet leisurely midnight cocktail in Natchez.

But for some reason, these annoyances that would lead even the most genteel Southerner to outbursts of rudeness in New York City are taken in stride. That's Natchez for you. These days when I go to Natchez, I go to marvel.

If one bit of local flavor best captures her romantic spirit, it is the descriptive, euphonious names of her houses—White Wings, Rosalie, The Briers, Myrtle Terrace, D'Evereux, Landsdowne, Cottage Garden, Hope Farm, Hawthorne, Oakland, Green Leaves, The Elms, Mistletoe, and of course, Dixie. These houses were built by visionaries, dreamers of an earlier time, and they have endured.

Just who were their builders? Ask any descendant of an "old planter family," as they call their aristocracy in Natchez, and you'll learn that originally "everyone came from somewhere else."

First Spanish explorers, and then French colonists, came to this beautiful, bountiful land named after the sun-worshiping Indian tribe, the Natchez. Eventually the British claimed Natchez, but in 1781 Spanish settlers once again seized the land. The end of the eighteenth century also brought many Easterners (though we would call them Southerners)—sons of the British who had settled first in Virginia, Georgia, and Alabama—who, like their pioneering ancestors, were seeking their own fortunes.

By the time Mississippi became a state in 1817, Natchez was a blend of old European tastes and cultures and new American ways and spirit. Despite their varied backgrounds, everyone shared a common thirst for adventure and wealth.

Plantations were already springing up by the 1830s, when steamboats and cotton made Natchez a center of lavish wealth, elegant sophistication, and, of course, boundless Southern hospitality. In a word, Natchez and the surrounding plantations "had it all."

When they made their millions, and they did, these voyageurs returned to New York and Europe to buy the finest furnishings for their Natchez showplaces. For their twenty-foot-square rooms with ceilings that rose to one-and-a-half-stories high they bought festooned cut-crystal chandeliers in France. For their formal parlors that often had not one, but two, massive fireplaces, they ordered exquisite Italian Carrara mantels adorned with classical themes. To reflect their Belter furniture imported from New York, they chose ornately carved and scrolled gold-leaf mirrors, palatial in size and feeling. Scenic wallpaper and deep-fringed silk damask or velvet draperies added finishing touches to their formal rooms. And only English silver and French porcelain were good enough for their banquet-size dining room tables.

...as her timeless customs and magnificent and varied architecture attest.

Here's to the Fox

*There is a comradeship among hunters that has always
seemed to me one of the finest human relationships.*
Archibald Rutledge

Would you rather go chase a fox or ride to the hounds?
Ah, the romance of the Southern hunt—fox hunt, that is,
never to be confused with deer or duck hunting, or heaven forbid, a turkey hunt!

Few scenes are more theatrical or colorful than the gathering minutes before the chase begins. It is as if an eighteenth-century British hunting scene has stepped down from a canvas and sprung into life. Red-coated, black-hatted, white-panted, and leather-booted riders are strikingly handsome on sinewy horses, whose coats gleam from tireless brushing. Restless hounds, anxiously pacing the dewy ground, dart about. The rolling green hills and the fox await. The colors, the textures, the sounds, the smells, the excitement, the suspense are all there.

Robert Brooke is said to have brought this English tradition to southern Maryland in 1650, when he arrived with his family, twenty-eight servants, and his hounds. The gentlemanly sport was a great favorite even among the ladies, and Martha Washington occasionally enjoyed a hunt.

But we know that just as important as the hunt was the hunt breakfast, and the drink—measured and drunk from stirrup cups adorned with a likeness of the elusive fox.

Despite all this worldly grandeur, Natchez remained a place of untouched natural beauty, a charm that many thought was unsurpassable, unequaled.

Samuel Grier, a brilliant young Philadelphian who moved to Natchez in 1842, put it most eloquently. *Just imagine yourself on some warm sunny day, you leave Natchez, ride along a road on which a stone was never seen, lined on either side by a hedge of roses. The warm and gentle breezes from the sunny Southern seas come rustling through the trees which makes the atmosphere the most delicious in the world. After riding 6 miles on this road you enter a grove of Magnolias whose foliage is so thick that it bids defiance to the penetration of Old Sol's rays. Pass through this then enter a cotton field containing some 600 or 800 acres—across this you enter another grove of Magnolias through which the road winds in a serpentine course until it terminates at the renowned place of Elgin. Take your stand on the Gallery and you behold before you a place on which Nature has been peculiarly lavish of her gifts. At some distance in front you behold the garden yet in an embryo state, but which promises to be lovely beyond description. You also command a view of two or three of the neighboring plantations with their immense cotton fields. Here and there interspersed with the dark, umbrageous Magnolias. Within doors you discover Elgin to be the abode of a little Hebe whose joyous laugh and bright blue eyes greet you wherever you go. Such is a very imperfect description of Elgin, the place where I spend my time so pleasantly. Perfectly happy and free from care as a "Mountain Child."*

The Civil War changed this idyllic life. Union troops came. Wealth and leisure vanished. Death and sadness touched everyone. Yet most houses and their priceless furnishings survived. Ironically, Reconstruction destroyed more fortunes than had war.

Land, homes, jewelry, antiques, art, books were sold to pay Confederate debt taxes. Survival was more important than cotillions. Yet Natchez survived remarkably intact, even if her golden glory was tarnished, her carefree days gone.

Luckily, no new money crops or industries

came to Natchez at the end of the century, the way tobacco and textiles came to Virginia and North Carolina. And so this deep South town perched atop a high bluff retained much of her antebellum beauty. There simply was no money to build anew. Natchez, as she proudly reigns today, is the fulfillment of the prophecy "preservation by poverty."

But the people of Natchez never lost

This antique English mahogany butler's tray with sterling silver pitcher and goblets sit on an etched Sheffield tray in a Natchez plantation dining room.

their dreams. They never discarded the past. How could they? What memories they had!

Rachel and Andrew Jackson were married there in 1791. Lafayette was guest of honor at Hawthorne in 1825. Jenny Lind, the great "Swedish nightingale," sang there in 1851. Aaron Burr, Henry Clay, Jefferson Davis, General Ulysses S. Grant, even Tyrone Power, the English actor and great-grandfather of America's matinee idol, all had come to Natchez. Wouldn't *everyone* want to visit Natchez?

Yes, decided Katharine Grafton Miller of Hope Farm Plantation in 1932, and so, in the depths of another black era—the Depression—the Natchez Pilgrimage began.

Plantation homes, many still shabby in those days, were dusted off and spiffed up. Darkened, overgrown gardens were pruned and manicured. Once again massive doors crowned with beautiful fanlights swung open to grand entrance halls. But this time they opened to tourists, paying guests, who wanted to glimpse "the way it was." Once again the world came to Natchez.

The new money those tourists brought to Natchez was important then. It still is today. But when you're in Natchez and pay for your tickets, along with your tour of the old homes with their lyre-shaped punkahs and imported French china, displays of eighteenth-century English silver and grand American Empire and Victorian furniture, you also get something that money just can't buy—a sense of Southern hospitality that flows naturally when you love to share legends, beauty, history, and time-tested traditions with others.

What? Haven't been to Natchez? Well, you must! That's where the Old South still lives.

A Day in the Life

*"We had breakfast at ½ past 7, dine at 3
or half past, and take tea at 7 o'clock."*
Edwin Hall, Albemarle County, Virginia,
March 1837

~

There is no pastime more pleasurable to
me than curling up with a diary from long ago.
I love to read the personal glimpses of places
and people that others took the time to write
down, memories they preserved for us. Reading their descriptions, sharing their experiences, I realize that the past is not just a
bygone time. The past belongs to the present.
It lives in each one of us.

The time I spend reading these old journals is a dreamy time. I stroll beside Mrs.
Oakly on the Carters' James River plantation
in 1774 as she enjoys the crisp morning air. I
become Frances Anne Kemble seeing for the
first time the snowy white sands of St. Simon's
Island along the Georgia coast in the 1830s.
I am an excited Varina Howell Davis boarding the grand *Magnolia* steamship the week
before Christmas in 1843 to attend the plantation parties upriver.

And I never close a journal without real-
izing that no matter how different our times
may be, humankind's hopes, dreams, and feel-
ings never change through the years.

So when people ask me, "Just what would
a day in the life of a plantation really have
been like?" I yearn to reply, "It was a day just
like your day today—a day filled with little
tasks and big jobs, laughter and sadness, a few
grand moments, but mostly life's routine."

That isn't very glamorous though, nor
does it capture the flavor of Southern plantation days for the privileged people of the
time. But the diaries do. So here, for you to
curl up and read, is a simple passage that tells
a little something about a long-ago and far-
away day in the life of one segment of our
Southern ancestry.

Remember, though, this was written in an
era when time, real time— minutes and
hours—ebbed and flowed to pulses we are not
mindful of today. Sunrise and sunset, the seasons and the climate—not buttons, flips, and
switches—marked the passage of days and
years, of life.

Some might say that life in 1815 at Monticello was the same old, same old. Then, as
during the eighteenth century, the day began
around seven-thirty or eight with a hearty
breakfast, followed by a midafternoon dinner,
and ended with a candlelight meal, sometimes
no more than a "tea."

*The ever inviting
and gracious tea
table at Sherwood
Forest set with silver
and china belonging
to the famed
Tyler family.*

*As old Man River
rolls past Natchez
(opposite), a golden
calm settles across
the horizon. Drink
it in! No wonder the
gracious, leisurely
ways of the South are
extolled world-wide.*

Sound monotonous? Not to me. Sound inviting? Yes. It makes me yearn for the now-lost leisure and serenity that once marked a gentleman's or a lady's life. Such a day in the life at Monticello seemed to mirror the ever-watchful, timeless tranquility of the Virginia hills that enfolded and protected the house itself.

"Everything is done with such regularity, that when you know how one day is filled, I suppose you know how it is with the others," George Ticknor wrote about his visit to Mr. Jefferson's home. "At eight o'clock the first bell is rung in the great hall, and at nine the second summons you to the breakfast-room, where you find everything ready. After breakfast every one goes, as inclination leads him, to his chamber, the drawing-room, or the library. The children retire to their school-room with their mother, Mr. Jefferson rides to his mills on the Rivanna, and returns at about twelve. At half past three the great bell rings, and those who are disposed resort to the drawing-room, and the rest go to the dining-room at the second call of the bell, which is at four o'clock. The dinner was always choice, and served in the French style. . . . At about half past ten, which seemed to be their usual hour of retiring, I went to my chamber, found there a fire, candle, and a servant in waiting to receive my orders for the morning, and in the morning was waked by his return to build the fire."

That passage brought back memories of a conversation I had with Nancy Hale over thirty years ago in the shadows of those same Virginia mountains. Nancy Hale was a distinguished woman and an accomplished writer. Her finest book, *The Life in the Studio*, described her New England heritage and grow-

ing up as the only child of remarkable, artist parents, Philip and Lilian Wescott Hale.

I met Nancy Hale soon after her husband, Fredson Bowers, was appointed chairman of the University of Virginia's English Department. She was a formidable woman. I was a timid graduate student. Our cocktail-party conversation was, at the best, strained, until she asked me where I was from. "Danville, Virginia," I replied.

"Oh!" she exclaimed in warm, even awed, tones. "I've been there. I've been a guest there. The people in Danville live so, so *graciously!*"

What was a day in the life of the educated, privileged Southerner? It was a gracious way of life that we Southerners still love.

Could we recapture the truly old plantation days? Of course not. Who, after all, would give up our telephones, televisions, and closets! But it is fascinating to read about those long-ago days and to reflect upon the best of them.

~

"At eight o'clock you take your seat at the breakfast table of rich mahogany—each plate standing separate on its own little cloth—Mr. Carter will sit at one end of the table and Mrs. Carter at the other. . . . After breakfast visitors consult their pleasure—if they wish to ride, horses are ready at their command—read, there are books enough in the Library—write, fire and writing materials are ready in his room. The Master and Mistress of the House are not expected to entertain visitors till an hour or two before dinner, which is usually at 3."
Henry Barnard, from Petersburg,
March 1833

At Point of Honor in Lynchburg, Virginia, tea is served from an English tea set (top), while at the Beauregard-Keyes house in New Orleans it is kept warm in a French veilleuse (above).

Do Drop by for a Visit!

*"They seem upon the most friendly terms—
are constantly interchanging visits, without ceremony
or invitation; and their hospitality to strangers
is not surpassed in any country that I have seen."*
The Honourable Charles Augustus Murray,
traveling in the South in 1834

There's a tradition in Fort Smith, Arkansas, that goes back a long time in the South and knows no state boundaries. My friend Ed Dell Wortz reminded me of it when she asked, "See that flag over there?"

Down a ways along the banks of the Arkansas River that winds through this friendly town I saw a nautical flag flapping in the breeze.

"We could drop by that house and get a drink if you'd like," she laughed, quickly explaining, "When you run up the signal flag after five, that's an open invitation to your neighbors to drop in for a cocktail."

"Hope they serve sheep's-head hors d'oeuvres," I quipped. Then I told her about the old Tidewater Virginia custom I had read about in Susan Dabney Smedes' nineteenth-century journal, a sketch so colorful it is worth including here.

"Everybody kept open house; entertaining was a matter of course, anything and everything was made the occasion of a dinner-party. The country-seats were strung along the banks of the North River in a way to favor this. A signal raised on one could be seen for several miles up and down the river. If one of the colored fishermen, whose occupation was to catch fish for the table at the Great House, as they called their master's residence, succeeded in catching a sheep's-head, his orders were to run up a signal flag.

This was an invitation to dinner to every gentleman in the neighborhood. If a rabbit was caught, the same rule was observed. Rabbits were not common, which seemed to be the pretext for this, for they were not really esteemed as a dainty dish. A rabbit was served up rather as a trophy of the hunt than as a part of the feast intended to be eaten. But the sheep's-head in those waters were not uncommon, and one was taken by the fisherman of one house or another nearly every day. At five minutes before the time for dinner the gentlemen would ride up, or come by boat to the door of the house that had the signal flying. If any one was unable to attend, his servant rode up promptly with a note of regrets."

These days I'm sure no one sends a servant with a note of regrets, but I bet a few phone calls are made every afternoon in Fort Smith asking for a "rain check."

Everyone knows that Southerners make great hosts, but they also make great visitors. After all, it takes both to have a party. So through the years, some people have gone to any lengths to keep a steady flow of visitors in their homes.

The best account of an "open house" I've come upon is the tale of "Uncle Dick" and "Aunt Jenny" Cunningham, who lived in Culpeper County, Virginia, far to the west of the Tidewater region. Oh, and by the way, as Letitia Burwell, who told the tale, emphasized, that's Aunt Jenny with a broad, Virginia *a*.

"Uncle Dick had requested Aunt Jenny, when they were married, forty years before, to have on his table every day dinner enough for six more persons than were already in the house, 'in case,' he said, 'he should meet friends or acquaintances, while riding over his plantation or in the neighborhood, whom he wished to ask home with him to dinner.' This having been always a rule, Aunt Jenny never set her table without dinner enough for six more. . . ."

Now, that's Southern hospitality!

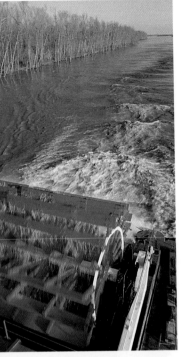

No matter how widely traveled you may be, the steamboatin' experience is one of the most enchanting.

Halcyon Days on the Mississippi Queen

"The steam-boats were literally floating palaces of ease and luxury. I have never seen any hotel where the food was so exquisitely prepared or the provision of dainties so great....A journey on one of the packets was an ideal mode of travel."
Varina Howell Davis, Christmas, 1843

Don't let her regal name fool you. She is as whimsical, or as majestic, as your own ephemeral moods.

One moment she is all aflutter. The next she is serene. She is nightlights and glamour. She is your hometown. She is cordon bleu. She is fried catfish. She is glitz and glitter. She is understated elegance. She is every woman.

Like all well-bred Southern ladies from any era, of any age, the *Mississippi Queen* caters to your whims—without compromising herself. She is the crown jewel of the greatest river in the world. She is Southern hospitality, and people from all over flock to her decks to savor her charm.

For Mark Twain and the legendary voices of the steamboating days of yore, it was adventure that beckoned to them. For me, a thoroughly modern, if admittedly sentimental and nostalgic, woman of the 1990s, it was the romance of it all that lured me to the *Mississippi Queen.*

Being on the road is one of the joys of my life. But after months of ceaseless car and plane travel, to say nothing of a different bed every night, I was ready to do something for me. I longed for a sense of home. I needed a feeling of permanence, even if it was only temporary.

I wanted to enjoy a leisurely sunset as the day came to an end. I wanted to be able to turn over in the morning, fluff up my pillows only to settle back down. I was ready to let Walter go by himself to get the great shot of the sunrise peeping over the horizon.

I wanted to see Vicksburg, Mississippi. It's on the road that veers off to the right where I've always turned left. I wanted to dock at quaint little St. Francisville, Louisiana, not skirt around it as I had done so many times in the past. I wanted to climb up the levee in front of Houmas House, one of just a handful of the great plantations still standing on the Mississippi River banks. And I'll admit it—I wanted to learn a little bit more history, but not too much.

I wanted the freedom to pull on blue jeans by day and to don a long, flowing silk skirt at night. In short, I wanted to drift for a few days. I needed to float. I had read the *Mississippi Queen*'s brochures and I knew I could do all those things—I could go steamboatin'.

I boarded her decks in New Orleans and float I did—for a glorious week, a week I will always remember, a week when time stood still, a week I'll tell my grandchildren about one day.

There's a timeless story about the fellow who booked passage on a steamboat from Natchez to New Orleans. Once there, he continued on to St. Louis, and then he bought a ticket back to New Orleans. Finally the cap-

tain asked if something was amiss. Harnett Kane, who repeats this legend in his book, *Natchez*, ends the tale with the mysterious passenger replying:

It's the finest way to pleasure myself that I know. No hotel in America can equal this. The finest food—your wild game, your glazed fish, your roasts, sauces and pastry! My cabin—it's as finely equipped, as well decorated, as any room I've enjoyed in my life. The bar, the cabin, the promenade—nothing to match 'em, I tell you. And the company! I meet all my friends, the best people in the world. Why should I want to leave?

Once you have tasted her life, no one ever wants to leave the *Mississippi Queen*. In fact, I met several people aboard who had taken the cruise from New Orleans to Natchez and back, once, twice, and one fellow who must have descended from the legendary passenger. He was on his seventh jaunt!

It took no time for us to make instant friends with the Fortes from D.C., the Hunts from Phoenix, the Hugheses from Boston, Anne Pitman from Walnut Creek (California, of course), and Bob and Dorothy from Longview (Texas, of course). We were all well traveled. Worldly people, some might say. Among us we had crossed oceans, flown over the North Pole, seen the pyramids, climbed Asian mountain ranges. But the *Mississippi Queen* brought us together for a memorable trip on the lifeline of our own country—the great Mississippi, the river that Mark Twain said "is well worth reading about."

But the *Mississippi Queen* is also worth reading about. Today some people think that she and her sister vessel, the *Delta Queen*, are dinosaurs—that they have lived beyond their day and are doomed to extinction.

Never! For romance and wanderlust do not fade; nor do people who love to serve and who take pride in adding joy to others' lives. Now that I have ventured up and down that legendary river, I am sure that no single stretch of waterway has known more laughter or more tears than the ever-changing miles of the Mississippi. The great flood of 1993 attests to that.

Yet while we marvel at nature's unconquerable power, we need to remember that in 1896, almost a hundred years earlier, Mark Twain wrote, partly italicized, in *Life on the*

After a full day spiced with lively conversation and an adventuresome visit to historic St. Francisville, we pulled away from the shore. It was a magical moment at the end of a day on the great Mississippi River, which will live forever in my dreams and in my heart.

Opposite: From its luxurious staterooms (top), to its graceful deck (bottom left), to its elegant dining room (bottom right), The Mississippi Queen offers the best of Southern hospitality.

"Cordial hospitality is one of the characteristics of the Southern people."

John Anthony Quitman, of Rhinebeck, New York, writing from Natchez, Mississipppi, August 12, 1822

Mississippi, "*Nearly the whole of that one thousand three hundred miles of old Mississippi River which La Salle floated down in his canoes, two hundred years ago, is good solid dry ground now. The river lies to the right of it, in places, and to the left of it in other places.*" Yes, ole man river just keeps rolling along, at his own pace, in his own rhythm, to his own time.

But life aboard a Mississippi paddlewheel boat never changes. Centuries come and go; the river's path changes; the boats themselves disappear; but not the Southern hospitality you encounter once you give yourself over to the steamboatin' experience. It is a charmed life, a once-in-a-lifetime chance to live out your Huck Finn–childhood dreams in a Rhett Butler world of grown-up luxuries and extravagances.

There is the finest food. Wouldn't you know I would begin my praises with the food! Why shouldn't I? I'll always relish the variety of hearty seafood soups served piping hot and as grand as you'll ever taste. I could hardly find the broth for the chunks of oysters or crab swimming before my eyes. After two ample servings (yes, they really do honor your every request), I had to skimp on the other courses—to save room for the desserts, of course.

There is impeccable service. How could a passenger not smile when everyone you encounter who is attending to you is cheerful and accommodating? It may seem unbelievable, but I never heard one cross word or complaint during our entire week's cruise. From our delightful chambermaid, Julie, to our sprightly waiter, James, we found an endless source of goodwill and charm.

There is polish. Metaphorically speaking, the *Mississippi Queen* is a lullaby of a hotel. More than your resting place, she is your com-

fort. She is your cocktail lounge one moment, your coffee house the next. But always she is your safe harbor from dock to dock. She is your home, your haven, your escape, your little corner of paradise.

And there is not one inch of her tiers and decks where you cannot find beauty if you look. Her plush carpets and twinkling chandeliers are ever feminine, elegant, and flattering. Her gleaming brass rails and strong ropes are masculine, rugged, and necessary.

Like every woman, she is ever thrilling. Her throaty calliope is frivolously brash. Her moonlit nights are your dreamed-of kisses—gentle, never-ending promises. Her ambiance is the best of yesterday, the best of today.

Why should I want to leave? I didn't. Still, I had to. But I left with more. I have my wonderful memories. They will be with me tomorrow.

And, oh yes, I wore my jeans by day and my long, flowing silk skirt at night. That is what Southern women who have had the delight, the joy, the pleasure of being a guest on a resplendent Mississippi paddleboat have done through the years. Neither they, nor I, ever felt lovelier, and we loved every minute of it!

It seems only appropriate that my recounting of these memories of a few halcyon days of Southern hospitality aboard the *Mississippi Queen* be brought to a close with this heartfelt toast that our Captain Shewmaker drank to us our last night on board:

Here's to you all!
We want you to know our sentiments
are honest and real.
May your days be as bright,
And your hearts be as light,
As the spray from an old paddlewheel.

River Food

What do you eat when you're on the river? River food, of course. It's what everyone wants. It's a Southern tradition.

The kitchens on the paddleboats of yore weren't equipped with modern refrigeration, so passengers might glimpse a grubby hunter standing by his catch, a deer or other game, hanging up in a tree along the shore. A quick stop and the cooks could gather meat and fish for the day's meals.

Most people agree. They'd rather see maitre d' Barney D'Angelo's smile and feast on specially prepared dishes than eat raw game and fish. This is one case where the tradition has been improved with time. Here's a recipe for typical Mississippi Queen fare:

SALMON LA FOURCHE
Serves 10

Char-grilled salmon, crowned with shrimps, oysters, and mushrooms in a seafood wine sauce

> *1 pound medium shrimp, peeled and deveined*
> *1 pint shelled oysters in their liquor*
> *1 quart seafood stock*
> *1 ounce margarine*
> *1 ounce minced shallots*
> *1 pound sliced mushrooms*

Cornstarch or arrowroot
1 ounce Chablis wine
5 pounds salmon fillets (8 ounces each)
½ ounce lemon juice

1. Poach shrimp and then oysters with their liquor in lightly simmering seafood stock. Do not overcook. Remove shrimps and oysters to side containers, and keep warm by covering with warm seafood stock.

2. Heat margarine in skillet, add shallots, sauté briefly, and add mushrooms and sauté until lightly done.

3. Add remaining seafood stock to skillet and bring to boil. Mix cornstarch or arrowroot to Chablis wine and blend with stock to achieve a lightly tightened sauce with a nice sheen.

4. Meanwhile, finish cooking the salmon fillets in the oven. Do not overcook. If you wish, you may mark them on a charcoal grill before the oven cooking.

5. To serve, crown each finished fillet with equal portions of shrimps and oysters. Pour approximately 3 ounces of sauce over each serving.

In the 1920s, Lyle Saxon wrote about the plantations that had "vanished into the Mississippi" years earlier. Few grand houses are to be found along those ever-shifting banks these days, but the nearby towns and inland roads are dotted with beautiful homes and gardens that welcome visitors to their doors. We visited the St. Francisville Inn (top), Catalpa Plantation (near right), and Elgin (far right).

Her love for this land with its softly rolling hills of bright-red soil, this beautiful red earth
that was blood colored, garnet, brick dust, vermillion, which so miraculously grew
green bushes starred with white puffs, was one part of Scarlett which did not change
when all else was changing. Nowhere else in the world was there land like this.
MARGARET MITCHELL, GONE WITH THE WIND

No Other Land Like This

Ask a Southerner, "Just what color is the sky?"
and you'll learn something about the person you're speaking to. ⌒ "It's azure blue, that sort
of indescribable blue-green color of the ocean," my friend from southern Florida told me. ⌒
"Really! You're from North Carolina. You *know* it's Carolina blue!" a recent University of North
Carolina graduate chastised me. (Hers is the sporty car in the neighborhood with the bumper
sticker that boasts "If God isn't a Tar Heel, then why is the sky Carolina blue?") ⌒ "The
sky. Ahhhh, it's that rich blue shade of the Blue Ridge Mountain," a Virginian romanticized,

The beauty of the Southern landscape—crepe myrtles at Berkeley Plantation in Virginia (above), daffodils in a North Carolina garden (below)...

soil that runs from Piedmont Virginia all the way to Texas, or on the sandy-white beaches that stretch along the coast from Delaware to Key West.

Take a stand of majestic magnolia trees, their waxy green boughs tipped with ivory blooms, or a canopy of two-hundred-year-old olive-colored oak trees laced together by streams of silvery Spanish moss, plant them in Southern soil, drop a Southern sky behind them, and who needs a canvas? The picture pops off the page.

It isn't that the gray rock-bound coast of Maine hasn't a charm all its own, or that the rich black fields of Wisconsin are not lovely. They are. But under the intense crystal-clear Southern skies, the vibrant colors that dot the South's landscape gleam and shimmer.

Outside living is a part of our Southern way of life. We just grow up that way. Besides, being outside really is enjoyable through most of the South for at least nine, in some places even twelve, months of the year. (The less-pleasant months are the ones when it is too hot rather than too cold.) That's why Southerners have used their sprawling yards as an extra room since colonial times.

Before today's indoor, air-conditioned life-style, a thick carpet of grass sprinkled with patches of furry moss, cooled by late-afternoon breezes, and shaded by thick, primeval trees, was a heavenly place—the perfect setting for a ladies' tea, a solitary place to read a book, a playroom for rambunctious children, a refuge from the world as well as the heat.

Under the stars and moon, the same setting became transformed into a romantic hideaway. Long before nighttime lighting became popular, glowing white flowers were resplendent in our grandmothers' gardens.

pointing west. (Virginians always romanticize.)

So what if their "blue skies" are colored by their deep-rooted regional loyalties? All Southerners agree on one point: Their *Southern* skies are notably bluer than those elsewhere—particularly on a cloudless day when the dazzling sun shines down on the brick-red

With edgings of white candy tuft, spires of snow-on-the-mountain, clumps of Star of Bethlehem, and clusters of moon-kissed vinca to guide the way, who could resist the lure of Southern night air?

The out-of-doors was still all of those things in the 1940s and '50s when I was growing up, first in central North Carolina and then southside Virginia—a stone's throw from the North Carolina state line. In my child's heart and mind my own backyard was a hallowed, secret place where I acted out my dreams. And when one of Mother's friends held a garden party and I was invited, the backyard became a festive, picture book pretty, living place.

One afternoon I will always remember. This garden party was held at a grand estate in Pinehurst, North Carolina, a place famous for its horses, golfing, and the Yankees who came there. Mother and I, with throngs of other guests, were greeted at the front door. Then we were paraded through the house out onto a long, lattice-covered brick patio. The scene was wondrous. I had never seen such splendor before in real life.

Beautifully arranged serving tables were draped in flowing cloths that fell in great folds to the ground. Monumental (at least to my eyes) silver punch bowls, their frosted sides sparkling in the dappled afternoon light, flanked glorious, overflowing flower arrangements in elegant champagne urns. Candy mints in irresistible rainbow colors were everywhere. I was awestruck—when suddenly the unbelievable happened. Our hostess, a grand, stately lady, her gray hair pulled back to show off her noble features, singled me out.

"Would you like to help pass the refreshments?" she asked me. Before I knew what

had happened, I held a round silver tray filled with exquisite flower-shaped ice creams in my little hands.

In the center, exquisitely formed, delicate pink and red ice cream roses were artfully arranged on a bed of real ivy and camellia leaves. Around the border were snow-white calla lilies with lemon-yellow throats. Each

. . . a farm tucked away in the Blue Ridge mountains (above), ever-whimsical sunflowers that bloom wherever the sun shines (below).

No wonder Southerners have such a stong love for and desire to share their land when it yields such bountiful beauty as this vineyard in eastern Tennessee.

ice-cream blossom had a tiny wooden green "stem" to hold it by. I thought they were the prettiest things I'd ever seen.

Everyone raved over the "ices," as they called them. "They can't be real!" "They're delicious!" "What flavor is this one?" "My cousin told me she had had these at a party in Richmond." "May I have another?"

Only after my duties were over did *my* turn come. Could any delicacy possibly live up to my ever-mounting expectations?

I nibbled at the petals of a red rose. A sweet, grainy raspberry flavor tickled my tongue. The vanilla calla lily tasted as smooth as it looked—milkshake creamy and rich— the best. Raspberry and vanilla ice cream had never been so delicious, never tasted so exotic. Nor had any day been so magical.

During my childhood these ices occasionally showed up, but only at the most special garden events. A few years ago when I was planning a garden gala, I wondered, Does anyone, anywhere, make them?

I had a difficult time finding anyone, anywhere who even *remembered* them! "I haven't thought of those in years," my friends told me.

Then someone said, "*That's* what my friend was trying to describe to me. She had some at a party not long ago. Somebody must be making them."

I began calling around. Richmond? No. Savannah? No. West Palm Beach? "You mean marzipan." "No, these are *ice-cream* flowers." "Never heard of them." Then one day luck was with me. "Yeah. You can get those out of Connecticut."

I was a little surprised and, I admit it, disappointed. All along my flower "ices" seemed to epitomize Southern hospitality. They weren't at all "Northern." But I had a phone number and a lead. I gave them a try.

Our conversation began something like "I'm calling from North Carolina. I understand you custom-make ice-cream favors shaped like flowers."

"North Carolina! I'm from North Carolina."

In no time at all Bunny Brown and I were chatting about mutual friends in Raleigh, Smithfield, and Kinston. Finally the conversation turned to the ices.

Yes, she, too, had never forgotten about the ices she had served at one of her mother's friends garden parties when she was growing up. But she had learned how to make them. Later, when she moved North, her Yankee friends insisted that she create them for *their* parties because they were "so very Southern."

That's the thing about our Southern ways. We remember the lovely and the special—the color of the sky and the land, the beauty of our gardens and the pleasurable hours we spent there—and our love for these things does not change, even when all else is changing.

A Bouquet of Stolen Sweetness

~

The Thompsons' white frame house with a silver tin roof looks more like it belongs in the country than on a busy corner in Danville, Virginia, where two three-lane streets intersect. The yard is certainly more country than town. That's why I usually slow down a few yards before I get there. I want to give the traffic signal at the intersection enough time to turn red so I can get a better look at what's blooming.

Plants and flowers are everywhere. Iron kettles filled with begonias swing from a free-standing pole in Mrs. Thompson's side yard. Bushy ferns and spiky philodendrons turn her front porch into a small jungle. Sky-blue hydrangea bushes bloom their hearts out from May until October. All in all, the Thompsons' Main Street house is a comfortable, never-changing landmark in this ever-changing world—with one exception. There used to be a blanket of gardenia bushes where the hydrangeas now grow.

A killing deep freeze swept through Piedmont Virginia and North Carolina at Christmas a few years ago. It didn't just nip the tender gardenia and camellia bushes that prefer the deep South to those Southern states farther north. It killed them, roots and all. That's when Mr. Thompson planted the hydrangeas. They are heartier shrubs, and their blooms last much longer.

But from years and years ago I remember Noel Thompson's gardenias. To me, a gardenia's velvety white petals and sweet pungent fragrance are irresistible. (I've never liked any of the gardenia-scented commercial fragrances—the perfumes and powders—though. They're too strong, too heavy for wearing indoors. But there's nothing more refreshing than a whiff of a freshly opened gardenia blossom's sweetness in the open air.) To me, gardenias are the most Southern of all the flowering shrubs of which we have so many.

Someone else agrees with me. For back when the gardenia shrubs banked the Thompsons' front yard, a traveler passing by the house early one June morning saw them, stopped the car, went over and picked a bunch, wrote an unsigned thank-you note, and left a five-dollar bill. Seems the unknown traveler had moved North and was on her way back home after a quick trip to visit Southern relatives. The traffic signal was red when she got to the Main Street intersection in front of the Thompsons' house. That morning, when the gardenia fragrance wafted on Southern breezes into her car, she couldn't resist swiping a sweet Southern bouquet.

The Thompsons called the newspaper, and they ran a couple of lines about the incident. That's what small-town Southern newspapers do.

I still remember Mr. Thompson's comment to the reporter. He said, "I'm glad she stopped and picked them, but she shouldn't have left the money. She should have rung the doorbell. I would have given her all she wanted, for free."

As welcoming as the homes, as varied as the people, the Southern gardens from Maryland to the Mississippi, from the seaports to the rolling hills, are lush and exuberant, quiet and romantic.

Every House Had a Porch

"In the evening when they walked about they found people sitting on the doorsteps of the dwellings, in a manner not usual in a northern city...."
Mark Twain

❧

There was a time—it seems only yesterday—when we Southerners watched life's parade from our front porches.

Our days began when the paper boy flung news from down the street and around the world onto our porch steps. Our days ended when "the man of the house" ceremoniously switched off the porch light and the household turned in for the night.

Like every Southern child of my generation, and those before, I grew up with porches—front porches, back porches, side porches.

A June baby, I first learned how to crawl, and then walk, up the front porch steps the spring after I was born. As a child I played with my dolls and made mud pies on the steps of the back porch, close to the kitchen so Mother could keep an eye on me. When I was a young girl, after we moved to another house, I tasted my first delicious kisses on the wicker couch on our side porch.

Then came the 1950s, air-conditioning, and TV. I can almost divide my life into two distinct periods, the years spent out on the porch and those spent inside.

My memories of the porch years are rich. They hold cherished sights, evocative smells, and familiar sounds of our neighborhood, recollections of the people who came and went, and, of course, conversations to last a lifetime.

My memories of the years spent inside are trivial. By comparison they are prosaic, one-dimensional, and predictable. There's a thin Andy Griffith, a perky Mary Tyler Moore, and now, I shudder to admit it, the sequined gown Vanna White wore last week.

The porch I most remember was the side porch on our early 1920s yellow stucco house

Southern porches are not just for rocking. Gentle Southern breeze makes meals more delicious at Indian Fields in Virginia (above) and afternoon dreams even sweeter at the McFaddin-Ward House (right).

on Marshall Terrace in Danville, Virginia. My family lived there from 1947 until 1963, the year after I married. But the porch years lasted only until 1956 or '57.

When the vacant lot on the porch side of our house was sold, my parents decided to close in the porch. They wanted a television set anyway, but they refused to put it in the living room.

The carpenters went to work. The delivery truck brought a twelve-inch GE black-and-white TV. The porch was closed in, and life was closed out.

No longer did I hear Mrs. Yarborough sweeping her troubles away as her broom rhythmically swished against the pavement. No longer could I smell the cotton-candy–sweet honeysuckle and mimosa waft by on velvety summertime breezes. No longer could I watch Bob Harper escape his mother's calls by crouching beside the cars parked along the street. Most of all, no longer did Mother have a living, breathing backdrop for her observations about life, vignettes best summed up by "In every house on every street in America there is a story waiting to be told."

We traded it all in for canned air and canned entertainment. Conversation became less important. Life lost many of its stories.

Twenty years later my children grew up watching MTV in air-conditioned comfort. But life has its little twists.

These days Langdon and Joslin both live in un-air-conditioned houses with front porches. Nothing amuses me more than to call one of them, let the phone ring until finally I hear "Hello? Oh, hey, Mom. Sorry. My friends and I were out on the porch."

After we've talked and I've hung up, I feel nostalgic. I miss my side porch days.

Anne Spencer's Garden

THE SOUL OF LOVE

~

Virginians tell you, Our gardens surpass all others. On a flawless Virginia day, strolling along the sweeping paths at Monticello, Mount Vernon, Virginia House, or any one of countless other public and private gardens, you might agree with them. Low-growing mounds of boxwoods intermingled with skyward-reaching magnolia boughs tipped with white blooms are luxuriant and beautiful.

Because Virginia's garden heritage stemmed from her English roots, we picture her gardens as formal settings—like carefully laid out and meticulously kept rooms. Yet no writer or poet has captured the transcendent glory of the Virginia garden with greater subtlety or gentle humor than the twentieth-century black poet, Anne Spencer. Her disarmingly unpretentious garden in Lynchburg was the inspiration for most of her poetry. Here for you to enjoy is her poem, "Life-Long" in which she compares Virginia's gardens—not England's—to heaven.

Life-long, poor Browning never knew Virginia,
Or he'd not grieved in Florence for April sallies
Back to English gardens after Euclid's linear:
Clipt yews, Pomander Walks, and pleached alleys;

Primroses, prim indeed, in quiet ordered hedges,
Waterway, soberly, sedately enchanneled,
No thin riotous blade even among the sedges,
All the wild country-side tamely impaneled . . .

Dead, no, dear Browning lives on in heaven,—
(Heaven's Virginia when the year's at its Spring)
He's haunting the byways of wine-aired leaven
And throating the notes of the wildings on wing;

Here canopied reaches of dogwood and hazel,
Beech tree and redbud fine-laced in vines,
Fleet clapping rills by lush fern and basil,
Drain blue hills to lowlands scented with pine . . .

Think you he meets in this tender green sweetness
Shade that was Elizabeth . . . immortal completeness!

During her lifetime Anne Spencer's home and garden were always open. In the days of segregation, Southern motels and restaurants were closed to even the most accomplished and notable blacks. But when traveling through Lynchburg, often on their way to or from New York, Marian Anderson, W. E. B. Du Bois, Paul Robeson, George Washington Carver, and Langston Hughes, to mention only a few guests, were treated to the best Southern hospitality at 1313 Pierce Street—good food, a comfortable room, music, and conversation.

Almost twenty years after her death at ninety-three, Anne Spencer's small but charming garden has been restored and is open to the public. There you stroll, not just among peonies, roses, wisteria, and violets, but among the gifts that others brought to her door—thank-you tokens given in appreciation of her generous hospitality. There is a statue of Minerva, a gift from a friend who admired Anne's wisdom; an African sculpture brought to her by W. E. B. Du Bois; her garden cottage, "Edankraal," a gift from her husband, Edward, as a retreat where she would write; and bulbs and flowers generously donated by Lynchburg gardeners as a fitting tribute to Anne Spencer's literary talents and loving, convivial spirit.

Country Roads

"Walter, what's your favorite picture?" I asked one sweltering August day when we were working in Washington and no longer on the road. ⌒ After a long silence and a pensive, don't-expect-a-definitive-answer look, he said slowly, "Probably one of the kitchen at Cross Creek." ⌒ "Oh, yes." I smiled nostalgically, for at Cross Creek, Marjorie Kinnan Rawlings' old Florida farmhouse, we found a quiet hospitality that comes from a genuine love for the celebration of life, a hospitality found only in the rural South. ⌒ You know you're in the real South when you pull over at a fork in the road at the Dew-Drop-In

Through a time-worn screen window, freshly picked fruits and simple kitchen things at Cross Creek are transformed into an exquisite still life.

A charitable, unreserved Southern hospitality lives deep in the vanishing countryside where people who just happen to be moseying along the same road at the same time greet one another with the forefinger of their steering-wheel hands. You find no strangers there. No horns honk. Nobody whizzes past you. You drift with the road. You are one with the rhythm of the seasons.

Over the past three years I've spent a lot of time journeying down country roads. I never would have imagined how much I craved to be on them, or how much of a part of me they would become. This didn't used to be the case. As a child living in a small North Carolina town, I dreamed about exciting city sights—neon lights, jukeboxes, sidewalks to skate on, and streetlights on side streets.

These days my older, city self seeks out quiet people and plain houses. More and more I need to bathe in softly filtered sunshine and undisturbed moonbeams that cast a blue glow on the earth beneath.

When driving along straight, high ridges, looking far into the distant horizon, I think to myself, No painting can equal the stark beauty of the endless stands of sharp-needled pine trees—trees made more green by the fall's occasional yellow-leafed poplars and red-leafed dogwoods.

While winding with the road up and down gently rolling meadowlands, I want to stop, to snap a mental picture of the weathered red tin roofs and graying timber fences to dream about all night.

I know that farmhouse over there, the one with the snow-on-the-mountain blooming alongside the zinnias and black-eyed Susans in the front yard. I know the dusty smell of that hay-filled barn that leans, each

or Ma Collins' Place to get a pack of Nabs and a Pepsi, and you end up sticking around to talk to people you've never met before and you'll never see again. Yet even before you get back in your car to drive off, you can predict that your just-for-a-moment new friend's parting words will be: "Come on back anytime you're out this way." You know you won't. And you wish you could stay.

I've given a lot of thought to why the people who choose to stay in these crossroads and hamlets, on the farms and rural towns, are so gentle and friendly. I watch them grin and I see their eyes laugh. I listen to their kindly gossip and their teasing banter.

Oh, it isn't that they have no troubles. They have more than their share. And they voice their worries—complaints about the factory that's moving in or the proposed landfill. These important issues threaten their homes, their way of life, which, when it comes right down to it, is why these unassuming people are so special.

They think where they are is best. It is home. They want to share their best with you.

These pictures of Marjorie Kinnan Rawlings' kitchen will be treasured by all who have read Cross Creek Cookery. And I hope those who have not may be inspired by the timeless descriptions of life and food that Rawlings so vividly depicted.

The hidden woods of Northern Florida became a writer's home and her sanctuary where she observed life's and the seasons' comings and goings and left a legacy for generations to come.

year, a little more to one side. I know those red kittens, and the red-headed little boy they're crawling over. These rustic sights never change. They are ever with me, for these are my familiar country road scenes through the Piedmont South—Virginia, North Carolina, South Carolina, and Georgia.

But the approach to Cross Creek on Florida State Route 3 is quite different—flat and, to my eyes, all one color of green. It is poor land, and the miles roll by unnoticed under your wheels. We traveled the road twice, once by night, once by day.

At night we crept along, not at all sure where we were, or where we were going. I kept telling Walter that we should turn back, that the road was dark and forbidding and ominous to city folks like us. Finally we turned around.

By daylight we came to Cross Creek once again. I was dubious. The sights did not thrill me. Where was the beauty Marjorie Kinnan Rawlings had extolled in her deeply moving books? Where was the countryside's freshness, its luminous glow?

We parked and began the short trek along the well-worn brown pine-needle path to the simple white clapboard house. A loud-voiced duck waddled by. A red-feathered rooster half flew, half strutted my way. The smell of fallen oranges, their citrusy fragrance seeping from the pin-size burrows made by birds and bees, filled the air. I heard the wooden back porch door creak, then bang shut. Suddenly all was golden and enchanting.

"I think I could live here," I told Walter, quickly adding before he could, "if the night didn't fall."

Many lonesome, eerie nights do fall in this forgotten part of north-central Florida. To outsiders, the darkness broken by threat-

ening winds and dark shadows is morose and terrorizing. To those who live there the nights are peaceful and soothing, a time of rest.

Marjorie Kinnan Rawlings sat at her desk on the screen porch, or veranda as she called it, and wrote of her Cross Creek.

Folk call the road lonely, because there is not human traffic and human stirring. Because I have walked it so many times and seen such a tumult of life there, it seems to me one of the most populous highways of my acquaintance. I have walked it in ecstasy, and in joy it is beloved. Every pine tree, every gallberry bush, every passion vine, every joree rustling in the underbrush, is vibrant. I have walked it in trouble, and the wind in the trees beside me is easing. I have walked it in despair, and the red of the sunset is my own blood dissolving into the night's darkness. For all such things were on earth before us, and will survive after us, and it is given to us to join ourselves with them and to be comforted.

And she wrote about the generosity and hospitality she found there, like the "pound party"—an old Southern custom my own mother often told me about—a party where everyone brought a pound, be it of butter, sugar, meat, flour, or a pound cake. And she wrote of the people, black and white, who lived there, like 'Geechee, a homeless black woman she befriended who returned her generosity to excess.

She cleaned my house. She began with the painted wooden ceilings, the hand-hewn rafters where generations of dirt-daubers had built their mud homes. She continued down the painted walls, where roaches had trailed and long-vanished children had drawn pictures. She included the furniture in her sweep, so that polished mahogany emerged pale and unshining. She washed rugs that would go in the washpot. Those that

would not, she beat until they hung limp and dust-less over the clothesline. She thrashed mattresses in the sunlight. Their tufting covered the yard like full-blown thistles. She ended with the floors. . . . I shall never have a greater devotion than I had from this woman.

And she wrote of the food she cooked. Marjorie Kinnan Rawlings' *Cross Creek Cookery*, first published in 1942, has never been out of print. It remains a gift of hospitality and words, good food and Southern scenes, memories and recipes.

In passing them on both to novitiate and to initiate, I wish that I might pass on, too, the delight of the surroundings in which they have been eaten. Whenever the Florida weather permits, which is ten or eleven months out of the year, I serve on my broad screened veranda. It faces the east, and at breakfast time the sun streams in on us, and the red birds are having breakfast too, in the feed basket in the crepe myrtle in the front yard. . . . At dinner-time, the sunset is rosy on the tall palm trunks in the orange grove across the yard. We have for perfume the orange blossoms in season, or the oleanders, or the tea-olive. We have for orchestra the red birds and mocking birds

and doves and susurrus of the wind in the palm trees.

In cold weather, we eat in the old-fashioned farmhouse dining room with its open fireplace. If there are only one or two guests, we are likely to have our winter breakfast on a small table in the living room by the roaring hearth fire, looking through the French windows out across the veranda to the fresh leafy world beyond.

We eat leisurely always, and sigh when we think it wise to eat no more. . . . Much of my "company" food is on the rich side, and I should not recommend some of the dishes for daily consumption. My friend Cecil reported to an acquaintance that after a dinner at Cross Creek, dripping with Dora's cream and butter, the guests often wandered through the old farmhouse and fell . . . on the beds to sleep. The acquaintance was horrified and avowed that such disappearances must be annoying to the hostess.

"Oh," said Cecil, "the hostess goes to sleep, too."

Yes, country Southerners have an especially generous style of hospitality. It stems from their belief that where they are really is best. And they give their best to you.

"Enchantment lies in different things for each of us," Rawlings reflected. "For me, it is in this: to step out of the bright sunlight into the shade of orange trees; to walk under the arched canopy of their jadelike leaves; to see the long aisles of lichened trunks stretch ahead in a geometric rhythm; to feel the mystery of a seclusion that yet has shafts of light striking through it. This is the essence of an ancient and secret magic."

The shores of the beautiful Mississippi (above) are hundreds of miles from the stately pecan groves of southwestern South Carolina (left), but along the country roads (opposite) that stretch in between, Southern hospitality is ever-present.

"Don't you get tired of being on the road?" I am asked. Of course, but the lure of country roads always wins.

A Country Fair

DEEP IN THE HEART
OF TEXAS

~

The hard-as-brick floor in the American Airlines Dallas–Fort Worth terminal isn't any softer than the floor in America's Chicago terminal. And without fail the trek from my incoming flight gate to my connecting flight gate in Dallas–Fort Worth is always a twenty-minute hike—much longer than my usual seven- or eight-minute walk from Terminal H to Terminal K in Chicago. But oh, what a difference there is between the two places!

Those differences aren't something that I dwell on or think about between flights. They just jump out at me when I'm in the two cities—like the other day in Chicago when I was dutifully walking in step with my fellow passengers down the terminal corridor.

Suddenly, right behind me, a gruff voice boomed in no uncertain terms, "Watch out. Coming through. Coming through."

As one, we all crunched against each other and the wall to avoid being run over by the dead-on-our-heels nine-passenger people-mover. The vehicle lumbered by, barely missing us. That was it. There was no "Thank you," no "Excuse me." Just "Coming through." Moving on.

Later that day, in Dallas–Fort Worth, the same thing happened. Well, almost. This time though, the squishy sound of the people-mover battery caught my attention first.

"Please excuse our cart," I heard next as the driver slowed down and waited for a break in the oncoming foot traffic before pulling around us.

"Thank you." He nodded as the cart passed by.

What is it about the South? I smiled, shaking my head in gentle amusement.

Looking around me, I saw big men wearing wide cowboy hats and saucer-size belt buckles and big women with tall hair wearing high-heeled shoes. People in Chicago make jokes about their types. But those big guys and women also wear big smiles and they are polite to a fault.

Along the corridor, in the airport storefronts, strings of red peppers, Dallas Cowboy and Houston Oiler T-shirts, Marlyn Schwartz's most recent book poking fun at Southern belles, and Lone Star banners shouted out at me, "You're in Texas and don't you forget it!"

That's the thing about Texas. You're never allowed to forget where you are. Know what? I don't want to forget. I want always to remember the hours I spent at the Fort Bend/Rosenberg, Texas, County Fair—always. They'll help keep me young and smiling.

Late September and early October is fair season in Texas. The breezes hold a hint of fall. The leaves have a rim of yellow. Summer's beaches are tired and Christmas seems a long way off. It's time to pack up the family and head for the midway.

That's what we always did, both when I was a kid and when my own children were in school. In Danville we even had an official "Fair Day," when school let out early. There was no homework that night and you could be sure your friends, their families, your teachers, and your neighbors would be there by mid-afternoon—come rain or shine—and stay for the fireworks.

A Southern country fair truly is a time of

"Did you see the sign on our mailbox?" Jane Barnhill asked me. "I thought we did well to find the mailbox," I laughingly replied since it was past midnight when we turned off the rolling dirt road onto her driveway. "Well, go see it now!" she commanded. This is what I found.

While some fair-goers stroll along the colorful midway, others whirl to the Texas two-step or wait for the next rodeo event.

clean, down-home, family fun. Babies in strollers doze while their youthful parents stroll along hand in hand, no doubt remembering how they had courted here only yesterday. Kids of all ages play the games, ride the rides, talk loud, squeal, and eat cotton candy, corn, and hot dogs.

That night in Texas there was the usual crowding and jostling about in the midway, especially around the food stalls, but more than once I heard "Excuse me, ma'am" said the way only a Texan can say it. And I watched as proud but weary grandparents climbed to the top of the stands to watch Bobby and Sue play in the band or compete in the rodeo.

Walter and I had checked in at the main

gate in the late afternoon. We agreed to meet at the rodeo pavilion "in a few minutes." Walter started out to get some midway shots. I headed toward the deliciously pungent smoky fumes of pit-cooked barbecue. I started talking to the apron-clad cooks and in a "few minutes" the sun was setting and the moon rising.

The grounds were much larger than I had thought and so was the crowd at the pavilion. I was ready to give up finding Walter when I spied the telltale tripod slung over his back.

"Walter! Over here!"

"Stay there," he hollered back.

Yes, even a city slicker like Walter hollers in Texas. He ran off to catch the small band of fair workers who had volunteered to track me down. When I learned how much trouble I had caused, I began apologizing.

"It's okay." Linda Harris laughed. "It's fair time. It's crazy time."

Maybe, but it's craziness at its best.

There's nothing like the sight of children no more than seven or eight years old—little girls, their ponytails flying, little boys, their cowboy hats bobbing up and down—breaking out of the stall on big horses, chasing a fast-running calf in the Tiedown or Breakaway competitions at the Youth Rodeo. And the flags and the music and the roar of the crowd make it all the more thrilling.

These kids ride in the rodeo for fun just the way their dads and moms did . . . and still do. After the kids' show, the forty-something husband-and-wife teams take the ring in the Team Roping events. The Texas life is the good life in this community long ago settled by transplanted Virginians, Czechs, Bohemians, and Hispanics. Together they rope, they ride, they work, they play, and they do the Texas two-step.

Outside the pavilion the band was just warming up. "It ain't Mardi Gras time." I laughed to myself, playfully slapping my blue jeans. Seven months earlier in Mobile when the music started it meant we had eight minutes or less to change from our street clothes into white tie and ball-gown.

White tie or blue jeans, ballroom or grassy field—what does it matter? Music and dancing only heighten our very human, festive spirit. Some slide, some step, some twirl, some sway—we all move to the rhythm in our own way—the pencil-thin girl, the bearded man, the gray-haired lady with her purse on her arm, the mom teaching her daughter how to follow, not lead, the dad, his arms full of

Please Don't Double-Park Too Long

I was in a small midwestern town to give a talk on one of the hottest July days I have ever spent. There was no close access to the auditorium door, and I had slides and papers and props to carry inside. The parking spaces in front of the building were full, but there were some empty spots along a side street. I wheeled into one when I saw why. NO PARKING, the sign proclaimed. Underneath, in smaller letters, was written "from 5 A.M. to 11 P.M. for snow removal. $25.00 fine."

"Come now," I said to myself. "It's got to be 100 degrees and it's the middle of July. It's not going to snow."

I unloaded my car and proceeded to give my talk without another thought to the no-parking sign.

Needless to say, a bright-red parking ticket awaited my return. Being a basically honest, law-abiding type, I drove straight to the police station.

"There's been a mistake," I laughingly began, and told my tale.

I ended up paying the $25 fine, but not without angrily scribbling across my check, "Paid in protest in mid-July!"

When I got back to North Carolina I wrote a letter and suggested that the people in that town take a lesson from Kilmarnock, in the northern neck of Virginia. There they have a sign that reads "Please don't double-park long."

prizes won for the children. What a glorious sight happy people make!

It's always great to be in Texas—that place that never lets you forget where you are—especially at a county fair in September. It was even worth having to go through Chicago to get there.

Grandeur Comes to the South

"Think about it, Walter," I said one night over supper. "The old, truly Southern homes and places we visit have a wonderful *joie de vivre*, but they're not really grand, not in the broad sense of the word. Now, The Breakers is *grand*. Biltmore is *grand*. You know who brought grandness to the South? It was the Yankees!" ⁓ "Emyl, just think about it," he replied in his usual quick, but this time gently mocking, way. "Location, location, location." ⁓ "And dreams," I added. "Dreams of warmth and beauty. But"—my smiles turned to sighs—"some were pipe dreams," for I remembered the worthless property deeds

The romantic beauty and hospitality of the Breakers has a cosmopolitan flavor all its own.

I had found among my Massachusetts grandfather's papers in the trunk I emptied to make into a toy chest for my Southern children. These were deeds of ownership to "housing lots" in the Florida swampland uninhabitable by life other than snakes, turtles, birds, and alligators. Who knows, they are probably filled in now and worth a great deal of money!

The lure of the South was so powerful that, during the early years of the twentieth century, con men—carpetbaggers left over from Reconstruction days—filled their satchels with beautiful pictures and falsified prospectuses and headed back North.

They had been South. They knew its charm, its irresistibility. They traded on it and sold worthless Southern property to their own kissin' kin.

Yankees who had not been South were gullible. They had read about this paradise—this Shangri-La, this Eden, this Utopia—all the exotic places people dream about.

It is "like stepping into one of the tales of the Arabian nights," the press quoted a turn-of-the-century visitor to Palm Beach as saying. The *New York Times* remarked that to find its genie, "the Aladdin of Florida, Mr. Flagler, rubbed his bank account, and Palm Beach sprang into being."

Society columns described out-of-this-world Southern parties complete with casbahs, tropical breezes, exotic trees, and passion fruit. Magazines ran photo features on Southern homes that looked like Moorish palaces and French chateaux with gardens filled with Italian fountains and piazzas, Spanish and Moroccan statues and ruins.

This was a romantic era, a time when all things foreign and mysterious were dreamed about and sought after. The American wealthy hungered to establish cultural shrines to themselves—that's what they had seen on their European tours—and they could have them, in the balmy, fabled South. Others had.

Biltmore House, the 250-room mansion built on a 125,000-acre estate in the 1890s by George Vanderbilt in Asheville, North Carolina, was proclaimed "America's Versailles."

Opulent, "gilded age" displays of wealth sprang up throughout the South. It mattered little that they bore no resemblance to the eighteenth- and early nineteenth-century elegance of the "old South," or, if you wish, the South before the war.

True, antebellum ladies and gentlemen of the James River plantations, New Orleans, Savannah, and Natchez loved fine things, and they indulged themselves and their fancies.

They bought furniture and paintings in England and Europe for their Dixie mansions. Their impeccable taste for fine wines and food was world renowned. They threw elegant parties that lasted for days. They even showed off.

But it wasn't until Northern industrial money began flooding the war-poor South in the 1870s that she took on such a cosmopolitan air. Soon the South claimed the country's greatest resorts and most extravagant playgrounds—complete with golf courses, stables, yacht clubs—made all the more attractive, of course, by that nowhere-else-to-be-found charm—Southern hospitality.

In the legendary Breakers' skylit Circle Dining Room, diners enjoy an old world elegance and grandeur beneath a Venetian chandelier and hand-painted scenes of Italian cities.

Perhaps the stories of two railroad men and the hotels they built best tell this Johnny-come-lately tale of Southern hospitality.

Henry Plant was a successful Connecticut-born and Yale-educated (until he dropped out) businessman when he moved South in 1853 for his wife's health. In Jacksonville, Florida, he put his Yankee ingenuity to work, made shrewd investments, and began developing this area's untapped potential. By 1880, with Northern money backing him, he established a Southern railroad empire with Tampa as the center. Fruits and goods from Florida, as well as from Cuba and other points south, now could be shipped north. Better yet, rich Northerners could come in style and with ease to the sunny South.

For their pleasure he built the legendary, $2.5 million Tampa Bay Hotel. No amenities were spared. There was an eighteen-hole golf course, tennis and croquet courts, a conservatory to provide fresh flowers, a boat house and any variety of pleasure vessels, a heated swimming pool and spa, bowling alleys, even stables and kennels. For diversion guests could even take a rickshaw ride around the grounds—but not, as legend mistakenly has it—*in* the hotel! For evening entertainment there were grand dining facilities, a salon and ballroom, as well as a billiard room and a drawing room for the ladies.

The hotel was elaborately furnished with French carpeting, stunning European porcelains, the newest Eastlake furniture. Though there was steam heat, most rooms also had a cozy fireplace to take the chill out of the early-morning or late-night northern Florida winter air. In fact, the exotically beautiful, Moorish palacelike 511-room facility was Florida's first completely electrified large

building. For these luxuries, the guests paid from $5 a night upward during the December-through-April season. By comparison, a six-day steamer cruise cost only $18!

Plant's empire was dispersed after his death in 1899 and the hotel was sold to the City of Tampa. Today the building is part of Tampa University, but in a few rooms restored to their 1880s splendor we can revel in a rare, make-believe trip back in time to this grand hotel.

Meanwhile, though, in those nineteenth-century years in the eastern part of Florida—St. Augustine, Palm Beach, Miami, and even Key West—Henry Plant's friend and co-investor, Henry Flagler, was building yet another empire.

Flagler, a high school dropout, journeyed South from upstate New York via Ohio, where he made his fortune as one of John D. Rockefeller's associates. Then, in the late 1870s, doctors recommended that he take his wife South for her health. Sound familiar?

The Flaglers were impressed with Florida's climate, but not her hotels and travel accommodations, so they returned north. His wife died, and upon remarrying Flagler chose St. Augustine for his 1883 honeymoon. This time he decided to do something to improve Florida's resorts. By 1887 he had built the immediately successful Spanish-style Ponce de Leon Hotel—also costing $2.5 million. The parallels between Flagler's and Plant's lives were indeed remarkable—including Flagler's development of an eastern Florida railroad system to link his hotel with the rest of the world.

Seeking still other investments, Flagler continued farther South. In 1893, when visiting the small island of Palm Beach, he re-

In the 1880s wealthy Northerners traveled by train to enjoy the luxuries of the $2.5 million Tampa Bay Hotel.

When Henry Flagler, builder of the Breakers, designed "Whitehall" in 1901 as a wedding present for his bride, Mary Lily Kenan, no expense was spared, no "modern luxury" overlooked. From the state-of-the-art bathrooms to whimsical "puffy" lamp shades to a private game room (opposite), every dreamed-for luxury was a reality.

portedly exclaimed, "I have found a veritable Paradise!" I imagine he might have also said, "Location, location, location."

Palm Beach must have seemed as much like a paradise then as it does now. On a romantic spring night when the graceful boughs of her palm trees sway to gentle ocean breezes under dancing stars and a radiant moon, this is a jewel of an island.

Flagler found a small hotel already was there. But the Coconut Grove, named after the trees the island farmers had planted when a Spanish ship carrying thousands of coconuts had wrecked offshore in 1878, was no match for Flagler's grand scheme. He would build cottages and one hotel on the Lake Worth side of the island and another, larger hotel on the Atlantic Ocean side.

The Royal Poinciana on Lake Worth was built first. Then came the Palm Beach Inn for

guests who loved ocean breezes and beach strolls. Of course, the inn became the more popular site.

In 1901 the now-expanded Inn was christened "The Breakers"—a name that almost a hundred years later still captures the romantic, undulating waves that gently break and quietly echo against the white sands of its private beach. That was the same year Flagler married for the third time, this time to Mary Lily Kenan, a member of an esteemed Wilmington, North Carolina, family, and whose relatives own today's glorious Breakers.

Fire destroyed the original hotel in 1925, twelve years after Henry Flagler's death. By now the once-grand Tampa Bay Hotel was no longer very grand, but Palm Beach and Miami were even more glamorous and alluring to the fabulously wealthy as well as the comfortably rich. There, movie stars, business tycoons,

Whitehall's "best" guest room is reflected in a graceful full-length mirror, a hospitable touch that any guest might enjoy.

At Graylyn in Winston-Salem, North Carolina (opposite), and throughout the South, the wealthy gathered the finest furnishings and amenities for their grand homes. What could be more pleasant after a scrumptuous dinner than a cup of coffee and friendly game in the Persian Card Room?

royalty, and socialites rubbed elbows with vacationing families. Everyone agreed: Palm Beach wouldn't be the same without The Breakers.

Flagler's heirs rallied together and opened an even more splendid resort. Its architect, Leonard Schultze, the designer of the Waldorf-Astoria, had declared that the magnificent site was "worthy of nothing less than an Italian Palace." So that's what he built almost seventy-five years ago.

Today at The Breakers, nineteenth-century Old World appointments—murals, frescoes, tapestries, gilded ballrooms, marble fountains—complement the newest, most up-to-date and plush high-style fashions in carpeting, fabrics, and accessories. At latest count, her international staff can converse with the hotel guests in seventeen different languages. After all, the fabulously wealthy expect every whim to be accommodated.

What sets The Breakers apart is a deeply ingrained Southern tradition always present in my explorations to uncover the secret of *true* Southern hospitality as it has come down through the years. It is, in a word, family.

The Kenan family—descendants of Mary Lily Kenan Flagler and still ensconced in North Carolina—call themselves the stewards of The Breakers, but all who work there call the Kenans their "family."

As I toured through baronial vaulted ceilinged ballrooms beneath the constant gaze of cherubs and the palacelike lobby that, when bathed in morning sunlight streaming through towering, twenty-five-foot-tall windows with a view of a glorious courtyard, has the aura of an ancient castle rather than a 1990s modern hotel, mine were usual fact-finding, journalist-type questions: How long

have you been here? How many repeat guests come each year? Isn't that Bob Newhart? Is there a slow season?

My questions were answered, yet I soon realized that my attentive guides really wanted to talk about the spirit and traditions of The Breakers rather than feed me numbers and facts. Their words came easily and naturally as, with deep affection and pride, they told warm, personal stories about three generations of caring, generous Kenans.

I heard charming tales about Kenan grandparents and children, practical jokes they have played on one another, and grand family occasions we all would have loved to attend. And always I heard how tirelessly the Kenans give The Breakers their time, energy, money, and affection.

I thought to myself, such a tour and conversation could never happen in a stock-controlled hotel, no matter *how* grand it is, no matter how many "stars" it can boast. Simply put, strong family ties really do still matter to each and every one of us.

Later, remembering my visit there—a time of splendor, pampering, and romance—I put all my impressions together, and this is what I concluded.

I'm glad the Yankees came South—and brought with them enough money to buy bits and pieces of European splendor and bring it here. We had what money couldn't buy—location and Southern hospitality, and a sense of family tradition.

That's why, at The Breakers, unlike any other place I know of, guests bask in a wonderful blend of European magnificence and Southern comfort, they luxuriate in the midst of Continental polish and Southern politeness. Now, that's *grand* hospitality.

Biltmore's striking, baronial facade (above) invites you to even more stunning scenes inside, upstairs, and down. Here we see the grand banquet hall and the kitchen (opposite).

America's Versailles

A FAMILY'S HOMEPLACE

"To say I am Biltmore homesick and miss everything terribly would be silly, so I will merely imply it . . . in the evening we looked at the photos of the place and had little ecstatic fits over each one. . . ."
Adele Sloan, writing in her diary on March 28, 1892, after a visit to her uncle's home

❧

It takes a wild stretch of the imagination to call Biltmore House "homey." But that is what George Washington Vanderbilt had in mind when he began planning his future home.

Fabulously wealthy Vanderbilt had traveled widely in Europe in the 1880s. Upon returning, his dream was to create a lovely American "country estate," a noble concept, for the English country squire's home symbolized the very best in life—cultural interests, wealth made from the land, love of family, and a hearty welcome to whosoever might come.

But such a home called for the perfect spot. Vanderbilt found it nestled in the beautiful Great Smokey Mountains where lush primeval forests and rolling sylvan hills closely resembled the English countryside.

George Vanderbilt hired Richard Morris Hunt to design a house that would charm and enchant his friends and family. Vanderbilt's English country estate suddenly became a French chateau. The style mattered little. The hospitality did.

Guests to the estate arrived after a leisurely twenty-four-hour ride from New York—especially those fortunate enough to come in Swannanoa, Vanderbilt's private train car—at the Biltmore village railroad station. In horse-drawn carriages they proceeded along a beautiful quiet mountain trail dotted with babbling mountain brooks and native wild- flowers and foliage.

Few sights are as stunning, as thrilling, as the final approach to Biltmore House. On a cloudless day when the sun floods down, her beauty is blinding. On a misty mountain day when a gossamer veil hangs heavy and gray, her mystery is exquisite. Biltmore was and is a glorious, breathtaking sight.

Indoors, thirty-two bedrooms awaited—along with a paneled billiard room, two-storied library, gaming tables set up throughout the house for a pickup game of chess, cards, or mah-jongg, an indoor swimming pool, a well-equipped gymnasium, a fragrant solarium, formal and informal parlors, a magnificent baronial banquet hall, a splendid breakfast room, and long, plush, tapestry-hung hallways perfect for lounging or wiling away a leisurely hour or so.

Outdoors, guests could spend time on the Loggia, by the Lagoon, at the croquet court, in the Italian Gardens, on the Bowling Green, down at the greenhouses or stables, or on one of the terraces overlooking vast "pastures." These outdoor "rooms" were designed by Frederick Law Olmsted to entice woodland deer and wildlife to wander about freely, thereby enhancing even more the natural charm of this made-to-order enchanted land.

With so many choices, how did a guest ever decide how to spend a day? Here, from Biltmore's archives, is a day in the life of a

turn-of-the-century Biltmore guest in this very grand setting.

8:30	Hot water brought upstairs for the pitcher and bowl in the bathroom.
9:00	Morning tea brought to the bedroom.
10:00	Breakfast in the Winter Garden.
11:00	Change into a walking outfit.
11:30	A stroll through the Italian Garden, the Ramble, and the Walled Garden.
12:30	Change into a luncheon outfit.
1:00	Lunch in the Breakfast Room.
2:00	Change into riding clothes.
2:30	Horseback riding from Biltmore House to the Lagoon.
4:30	Nap, rest, or read in room.
5:30	Dress for dinner.
6:30	Aperitifs served in the Second Floor Living Hall.
7:00	Dinner in the Banquet Hall.
9:00	String quartet in the Gallery.
11:00	Stroll on the Library Terrace.
11:30	Select book from Library before retiring.

After days, even weeks of such exquisite and indulgent luxury, the guests departed, journeying down the same lovely trail by which they came. First, though, each was expected to write a few words in the *Biltmore House Nonsense Book*. It is little surprise that many expressed great regret at leaving! Even as a lowly tourist, I have never left Biltmore without a little tinge of regret myself.

❧

"Bow to the beauty of Biltmore
Its terraces, gardens and farms
Look out past the silvery river
To its chain of mountainous charms."

"Gilded age" visual vignettes at Biltmore: a bouquet adorns the back of each lady's chair at dinner (above); gleaming copper brightens the breakfast tray (right).

Jefferson Hotel

THE BELLE OF THE '90S

The Jefferson Hotel in Richmond, Virginia, is grand—but not too grand. She's the sort of 1990s hotel where a string quartet plays during afternoon tea, but there isn't a white-gloved lady in sight. She is elegant but relaxed, dignified but not stuffy. That is her heritage.

In the 1880s, while Northern vacationers were headed far South for tropical breezes, Northern businessmen were discovering Richmond. The city had been left in shambles after the war, but tobacco, America's new

"habit," and railroads were bringing in new money and new men. Any Southern belle can tell you, both were (and are) very important.

Lewis Ginter was a Richmond financier who wanted his city to have the "finest hostelry in America."

His splendid Jefferson Hotel was the talk of the town when she flung open her doors on October 31, 1895. A Tiffany stained-glass ceiling, exotic, imported palm trees and intricate cast-iron columns, a life-size Carrara marble statue of Thomas Jefferson, and especially the Grand Staircase dazzled everyone.

An arched framework encased three flights of beautifully figured white marble steps. Halfway up the steps, on one wall, hung a huge mirror that reflected the gilded deco-

Where Richmond's loveliest belles once would promenade, today visitors and the natives alike enjoy another Virginia tradition— Sunday brunch at The Jefferson Hotel.

111

What could be more "Virginian" than a bowl of native-grown peanut soup served in traditional blue and white English Staffordshire china in an elegant, richly paneled dining hall.

ferson Hotel for plush parties to celebrate this fairy-tale wedding of America's favorite popular artist to his model, "the Gibson Girl." In no time, The Jefferson Hotel herself became known as "The Belle of the 90s."

The name was most fitting. The Jefferson Hotel was the perfect backdrop to showcase Richmond's own belles. Even though the Civil War was long over Virginians fervently clung to the idealized image of the exquisite Southern lady as a reminder of her glorious antebellum plantation era.

At afternoon tea, decorously dressed in finest laces, family heirloom jewels, and their own irresistible Southern charm, Richmond's loveliest eligible young ladies flocked to the hotel. They promenaded up and down the Grand Staircase in hopes of catching not just the attention, but the hand, of a gentleman suitable to their dreams and station in life.

But with passing time belles fade, and new changes come along.

In 1907 a renovated, enlarged Jefferson hotel reopened. The Grand Staircase was no longer enclosed. Now live alligators swam in pools around the base of Mr. Jefferson's statue. These were still legendary days. If in Richmond, you stayed at the Jefferson. Nine presidents, Scott and Zelda, Charlie Chaplin, Gertrude Stein, and Elvis Presley did.

And legends grew around the Jefferson. Two bear repeating.

The first is just legend. No, the Grand Staircase was not the staircase in *Gone With The Wind*.

The second is fact. Yes, Bill "Bojangles" Robinson, was discovered waiting tables at the Jefferson. Some say that if you're very quiet, in the wee hours of the dawn after an all-night party, you can still hear

rations on the opposite blue and pink wall. Imagine how exquisitely romantic the dramatic play of reflected color and light must have been in this covered dream of a staircase. These were the ravishing sights of Vienna and Paris, heretofore unseen in the South.

When Irene Langhorne, America's ideal of beauty and grace, charm and womanhood—and also a Richmonder—married Charles Dana Gibson, New York's bejeweled society journeyed to the gilt and marble Jef-

his taps echoing on the marble steps!

By 1980 it seemed that the Jefferson, herself, would be no more than a legend when her doors closed. But Richmond would not let her die. Now magnificently refurbished, once again this elegant belle is the talk of the town.

Everyone who goes to Richmond stays there. Palm trees still add a touch of exoticism to her stateliness. Mr. Jefferson keeps a watchful eye on the comings and goings of the guests from his loft perch, but without any alligators underfoot. And Southern hospitality is dished up at the famed Sunday brunch—a Richmond tradition that brings families whose grandmothers and great-grandmothers once graced, perhaps even playfully swished up the Grand Staircase, and who knows—maybe even married a visiting Northern businessman, and convinced him to stay in Richmond.

JEFFERSON'S SPOON BREAD

Serves 10 to 12

4 cups (1 quart) milk
7 cups whole cornmeal
1 stick (8 tablespoons) butter
1 handful sugar (about 8 teaspoons)
12 eggs, separated

1. Preheat the over to 375° F.

2. In a large saucepan bring the milk to a slow boil. Add the cornmeal and cook until the milk becomes very thick.

3. Add the butter, mixing it in as it melts. Remove the pan from the heat and add the sugar.

4. In a large mixing bowl lightly beat the egg yolks. Add the cornmeal mixture.

5. Whip the eggs whites until they form soft peaks. Gently fold the whites into the cornmeal mixture.

6. Place the mixture in a butttered, floured baking dish. (A souffle dish or loaf pan will work well.) Bake for 25 to 30 minutes or until well browned.

PEANUT SOUP

Serves 6

Peanuts have been grown in Southern states since the Civil War.

In fact, pigs raised in the town of Smithfield are fed peanuts, which provide a distinctive flavor to the hams that are known worldwide as Smithfield hams.

4 ounces clarified butter
4 ounces onion, finely diced
2 ounces celery, finely diced
2 ounces carrots, finely diced
3 pounds peanuts
1 quart chicken stock
2 ounces all-purpose flour

1. Heat a large stock pot. Add 2 ounces clarified butter, the onions, celery, carrots, and 12 ounces chopped peanuts. Sauté but do not brown. Add the chicken stock.

2. In a food processor, puree the rest of the peanuts into a paste and reserve.

3. Mix together the remaining butter and flour to make a roux. Add the roux to the chicken stock, to thicken it. Bring the stock to a boil and add the pureed peanuts. Reduce the heat and simmer for 1 hour. Strain and season with salt and pepper.

Tiffany stained glass, a life-size Carrara marble statue of Thomas Jefferson sculpted by Edward Valentine, pipping-hot spoon bread prepared by Executive Chef, Mark Langenfeld—these are the mementos, the traditions that Richmonders try to preserve for all to enjoy.

Arrived at Grove Hill. How enthusiastic the welcome from each member of the family assembled on the front porch to greet us! How joyous the laugh! How deliciously cool the wide halls, the spacious parlor, the dark polished walnut floors! How bright the flowers! How gay the Spirits of all assembled!

LETITIA M. BURWELL, remembering antebellum days

Friend, Come Under My Roof

Like many children who grew up in the 1940s, I didn't take many vacation trips. Daddy was overseas in World War II from the time I was eighteen months until I was four. When he came home, he and Mother took short trips together to get reacquainted after their long, life-changing separation. While they were gone, I stayed with my grandparents or aunts and uncles. ⁓ When the three of us did take trips, our adventures weren't so grand—at least not in today's glamorous jetting-about, luxurious resort-hotel terms. Mostly we visited family. ⁓ Mother's North Carolina relatives lived within a couple of

Vintage pineapple-motif wallpaper welcomes all friends and travelers to Susina.

"his ladies" would be comfortable.

It was a big house with a spacious front porch, a tall, steep staircase, and fireplaces—one in every room. The fireplace I most vividly remember was in the warm, friendly dining room where all the guests gathered for breakfast around a knotty yellow pine, double-tiered, lazy Susan table—the first such contraption I had ever seen.

Every morning it was piled high with grits (which I hated, but now eat to excess every chance I get), scrambled eggs (that rated only slightly above the grits), and stewed fruits. But there were also delectable two-inch-tall biscuits, their crusty brown tops brushed with golden butter. Other than the biscuits, the roundabout action of the table interested me much more than the daily fare. What fun it was to watch the plates and platters shuttle back and forth in front of my eyes!

Even at my early age I observed that table time conversation follows helpings. How food inspires everyone to conviviality! When a guest wanted the grits that were a full 180 degrees away from his plate, he would politely ask, "Would you please send the grits this way?" This opened the door for someone to address the person, either with a comment or a question, and so conversation would begin.

In those days tourist home guests were like we were—middle-class people in town for a few days or longer. They, too, were seeking a homey atmosphere and the companionship of others like themselves, new—if fleeting—friends to pass their days with.

That time, so long ago, came back to me four years ago while I feasted on grits and biscuits at Dunleith, one of the many always-genial bed and breakfasts (that's what we call "tourist homes" these days) in Natchez, Mis-

hours' driving time. Trips to Daddy's native New England were more exciting. Those were overnight train rides. But once we arrived at our destination, we stayed with our relatives rather than in a hotel.

Then, in 1947, our family moved from Moore County, North Carolina, to Danville, Virginia. Little housing was available after the war. Daddy moved first, then a few weeks later he sent for Mother and me. He had found a tourist home, as they were called then, where

sissippi, and a resting place on my *Southern Christmas* adventure.

"Would you please pass the preserves?" the most attractive lady sitting opposite me politely asked.

"Of course," I replied, quickly adding, "and where are you from?"

It worked like a charm. Carol and Darryl Eisner were from Westlake Village, California, and on their way to New Orleans. So was I. Two days later, on Christmas Day, we all had a memorable dinner together at the Pontchartrain Hotel. Of course, California and Virginia are two thousand miles apart, and we've only met twice, but Carol and I con-

tinue to drop one another friendly notes.

Now, when you have an engaging conversationalist like Walter to charm the other guests, you don't need to talk about the food to break the ice. Still, our meals at the many bed and breakfasts we visited on our trek were so delectable that the conversation invariably turned to food as one melt-in-the-mouth course followed another!

But that's what you would expect, for generosity and conviviality remain at the heart of the Southern way of life. The traditions of a comfortable bed, memorable food, and grand hospitality have been Southern trademarks since the very earliest days.

Warmed by the early-morning late February sun, tulip magnolias and Spanish moss beautifully frame this Greek Revival home, now Susina Inn, built in 1841 in South Georgia.

George Washington, who loved entertaining, dancing, and conversation, set the standard for true Southern hospitality at Mount Vernon. Stories tell us that Washington was such a genial host that his friends journeying by horseback or coach to Alexandria would often "hide" in the woods surrounding Mount Vernon until dusk drew near. When it was too dark to travel the last few miles, they would "appear" at Washington's door, knowing they would be feasted and graciously entertained, as well as bedded for the night.

Walter and I undoubtedly felt a little like some of those eighteenth-century travelers the night we happened upon Susina, a magnificent Greek Revival home on Meridian Road, about halfway—the back way—between Thomasville, Georgia, and Tallahassee. We started the day in Warm Springs at the Little White House. Shortly after lunch we headed south on Georgia state Route 85 through the spring-kissed rural countryside toward Columbus. Once there, we just *had* to stick around to catch the shadows the late-afternoon sun cast on the Muscogee River.

"Where to next?" Walter and I asked one another, not in words, but in an unspoken raised-eyebrow communication that served us often, totally in tune even when we were utterly lost. There were no interstates nearby to whiz us along. So while Walter began following the highway signs tacked up on the downtown telephone poles, I squinted at the minute letters on the atlas, letters as tiny as some of the crossroads towns themselves.

In those first spring days when the sun sets early by the clock, we pressed aimlessly on. Looking at the map back at my desk in Virginia, I no longer have the vaguest idea why we got off a red road onto a black one, though I'm sure it made sense at the time. But when we reached Donalsonville, Georgia, some decision had to be made.

Like the travelers lurking outside of Mount Vernon, we were in need of room and board. The difference was that they knew where to find theirs. We didn't.

I began looking for a phone while Walter was getting gas and pretzels. It was too windy to manage the stack of notes I had on slips of paper at a roadside phone. That was no problem. Being in the South, I thought nothing of popping unannounced into an office on a side street in a town I'd never been to before and asking Holly Swanner (her name was on a plaque on her desk) if I could make a few calls. "Of course," she said. Southern hospitality is everywhere, I smiled to myself.

Looking over the list of places we might try, I thought if we could make it to Tallahassee. But as happened so often on our journey, fate intervened. This place was full. That place too far away. But by the time Walter found me I knew just where we were going. We were going to Susina.

With a full tank of gas and new excitement, we struck out following telephone directions I had been given that went something like this: "You'll be looking for a sign that says Route 319. It will be on the right-hand side of the road. Now to get there, go on through Climax to Cairo—that's spelled C-a-i-r-o, but pronounced Karo. When you're on the other side of Cairo, find Route 93 and after a few miles start looking for Route 193—that's Meridian Road. Turn right. Susina will be on the right. You can't miss it. You'll get here before dark, in time for dinner." Just like Mount Vernon, I mused.

I guess we could have been there by nightfall, if we hadn't stopped at Whigham to check out the site of the annual rattlesnake roundup—which we'd missed by a couple of weeks, thank goodness! And if Walter hadn't turned around in the middle of the road for what seemed to be no reason at all.

Slowing to a crawl, we cautiously bumped along the overgrown dirt shoulder until he brought the car to a stop. My side of the car was almost touching the barely visible gnarled

Kirkwood, in tiny Eutaw, Alabama, is acclaimed as one of America's architectural masterpieces (opposite and above).

For those who wonder why such a magnificent home as Kirkwood was built in Eutaw–it was for the good life.

and rusty double-strung barbed wire fence running along the edge of the deep woods.

"Look," he whispered, flicking on the high beams. In the glow of our headlights, solitary in the beauty of the late dusk, an ancient marble crypt rose out of the wildness around it.

Spring had not yet touched this wooded place that had once been a family cemetery. But soon it would come. The one or two dried brown leaves still hanging to the bare oak tree branches silently linked season to season. For just a second our lights shone on a life and a time now gone, hidden away except for the occasional accidental visitor. "I don't think I would have seen it in the daytime," he said.

I was so glad he had seen it, though, for when you travel through the South and find these wonderful discoveries, you take a moment to reflect. It was when I saw this sight while on our way to another grand experience in Southern hospitality, that I remembered the inscription on an eighteenth-century Virginia tombstone,

Every worldly Comfort fleets away;
Excepting only what arises,
From imitating the Virtues of our Friends;
And the contemplation of their Happyness.

Our after-dark arrival at Susina really wasn't any problem. We found the almost-hidden sign. And since we were still full from our snacks, we were pleased to learn that dinner wouldn't be served until 7:30 or 8:00 P.M. —much like the ways of the plantation days. An even more pleasant surprise was meeting our hostess, Anne-Marie Walker. Don't let her double name fool you. She's Scandinavian.

It's hard to describe, even in a book, all I learned from staying at the various bed and breakfasts we happened upon on our journey. I'll begin by saying, though, that they're not for everyone. In fact, some nights it was necessary that we each be near telephones with computer modem capabilities, or where one of us could receive a fax or a Fed Ex package.

Other times one of us craved a TV, or an exercise room, to say nothing of a drink machine you could have access to at 2 A.M. These are the comforts of our own homes, the comforts of modern hotels and motels that not every bed and breakfast can offer.

But, oh, what they *do* have! There is real wallpaper on the walls—none of that speckled green and pink design that matches the striped heavy-duty, all-purpose wall-to-wall carpet that runs from the lobby to the fire escapes on every floor. And the guests who stay at b & b's travel in cars that are loaded down with bags of fruit and souvenirs they're taking home. These people have no planes to catch so they take the time to linger around to talk about where they've been, what they've seen, and where they're going next. And there are real hosts.

It is written of Baucis and Philemon, the Romans from whom the legend of true hospitality sprang:

*Architectual
splendors, rich
antiques, a piping hot
breakfast served to
perfection…this
is the hospitality
of Kirkwood.*

At Seven Sisters in Ocala, Florida, Victorian charm and grace is recreated by her owners to make visitors comfortable.

Breakfast at the Seven Sisters Inn

What is a bed without breakfast? In the cheerful but not-too-bright (for the slow to wake up) blue and yellow dining room we leisurely indulged in treats that were as lovely to behold as they were delicious.

If I could have had my way, I would have taken the niceties of the Seven Sisters Inn along for the rest of our trip. I did beg for Bonnie Marchardt's recipe for the blueberry French bread. It is perfect when served with a juice like a Ruby Red grapefruit or apricot nectar, fresh strawberries in sweet cream with a sprinkle of grated coconut on top, and an assortment of breakfast breads. Here it is. It's the closest I can come to sharing Bonnie's charm and hospitality with you.

BAKED BLUEBERRY FRENCH BREAD

1 loaf (8 ounces) Vienna bread
4 eggs
½ cup milk
¼ teaspoon baking powder
1 teaspoon vanilla extract
1 large box frozen blueberries (if fresh ones are not available)
½ cup sugar
1 teaspoon cinnamon
1 teaspoon cornstarch
2 tablespoons melted butter
¼ cup powdered sugar

1. Slice the bread diagonally to make 8 ¾-inch-thick pieces. Place the bread in a 10 x 15 oven-proof dish. In a medium bowl, whip together the eggs, milk, baking powder, and vanilla. Slowly pour the mixture over the bread, turn the bread to coat it completely. Cover the dish with plastic wrap and allow it to sit at least 1 hour, but overnight is best.

2. Preheat the oven to 425° F. Coat another 10 x 15 oven-proof dish with a nonstick spray. Place the blueberries, granulated sugar, cinnamon, and cornstarch in the bottom of the dish, mixing lightly. Wedge the slices of bread tightly on top of the blueberries, wettest side up. Brush the bread with melted butter. Bake in the center of the oven 20 to 25 minutes, until brown.

3. To serve, place the toast with the berries on a white china plate. Stir the remaining berries with a serving spoon to liquefy and then spoon them over the top of the toast. Sprinkle powdered sugar on top just before serving and garnish with a colorful flower.

The kindly hosts their entertainment grace
With hearty welcome and with open face;
In all they did you might discern with ease
A willing mind and a desire to please.

Southern bed and breakfast hosts and hostesses continue in that tradition. They are a rare breed, as worthy of high praise today as in ancient times.

Nature seems to have graced them with good spirits, generous hearts, multiple talents, and a liberal dose of eccentricities. They must always be smiling and cheerful, gracious and polite, even after rising by five o'clock or earlier each morning to feed total strangers.

Sometimes I think bed and breakfast hosts are the most talented people alive! They seem to be part historian, floral designer, en-

trepreneur, accountant, gardener, cook, maid, engineer, interior designer, antiques expert, and brilliant conversationalist, all rolled into one. They are highly energetic people—except when telling their guests good-bye. They never seem to want you to leave.

They love to celebrate the ceremonies of life—weddings, christenings, anniversaries, and parties, parties, parties. I think having guests for breakfast is a party in itself!

What amazed us, though, was how many of our hosts, like Anne-Marie, were not Southerners—at least by birth. Yet they had chosen to move South, and they have adopted our Southern ways. That says a lot. "You're a reconstructed Yankee!" Walter and I laughingly told them.

Walter and I also often talked about the

"Change? There is no change…. All of it is as it has always been," wrote Thomas Wolfe in Look Homeward, Angel *of "Dixieland," the boarding house his mother ran in Asheville, North Carolina.*

differences between Southern bed and breakfasts and those in other parts of the country. Certainly the trademark of all good b & bs is cordiality. But what makes the Southern bed and breakfast hosts different, I have decided, is the essence of Southern conversation—the distinction between a polite exchange and what I call "really getting to know you."

In other parts of the country people are cautious in their conversation. In the South people jump right in and ask you about your family, your hometown, yourself. They want to know whom you're kin to, whom you know—not because they are nosy, but because they're hoping they, too, know some of the same people and have been to the same places. Common experiences are personal, even intimate. Southerners care about those things that are important in your life. Sharing them is a warm, genuine way of becoming instant friends, rather than being another passing acquaintance.

So is sharing your home to make other lives more pleasant, more memorable.

❧

"There is nothing yet contrived by man by which so much happiness is produced as by a good tavern or inn."
Boswell's *Life of Dr. Johnson*

In 1894 the New Orleans Daily Picayune *extolled Jackson, Mississippi's Millsaps house,* "The walls are enriched with costly painting…bric-a-brac adorn the apartments." *Now, a century later you can also enjoy a Southern breakfast and bedtime praline at the Millsaps Buie House (opposite and below).*

Dinner at Monmouth

Even if you are not an overnight guest, you can still enjoy dinner at Monmouth. The night begins with drinks of your choice and an appetizer served on the veranda. When I raved over the praline sauce on the brie served with apple slivers, I remarked, "It's bought. It has to be."

Juanita Love, the chef, laughingly told me, "That's what everyone thinks, but it's not," when I asked where she bought it. "It's my very own." And when she shared it with me, I was ecstatic. The combination of the tastes and the distinctively different textures make this an unbeatable appetizer, or a very different cheese course—even dessert— Mississippi style.

JUANITA'S PRALINE SAUCE FOR BRIE

Dot ½ cup of coarse pecan pieces with half a stick of butter and sprinkle with sugar. Toast in a 300° F. oven for about 30 minutes, until brown but not burned. Set these aside.

THE SAUCE

1 stick (8 tablespoons) butter
1 cup brown sugar, packed
⅛ teaspoon lemon juice
¼ cup milk

Mix all the ingredients together and bring to a full boil. Boil until it reaches a fixed stage, approximately 3 to 5 minutes, stirring constantly. Please note that it does burn easily.

Next I asked for the secret to her salad dressing. She smiled and shook her head emphatically, uh-uh. But she did give me her recipe for French Zucchini Soup—a recipe for twenty people that she spieled off the way the old timey cookbooks do. When served as a main course for eight, I'll bet you and your guests will eat sixteen servings, and it's so good you'll want to finish up the leftovers the next day.

JUANITA'S FRENCH ZUCCHINI SOUP

A "tad" of chicken base (concentrated chicken stock)
¼ cup water
8 good-size zucchini sliced thin
1 cup chopped onions (Vidalia are best)
¼ cup chopped celery
2 cloves garlic, chopped
1 cup heavy cream
1 cup whole cream
¼ cup cornstarch
Curry powder
White pepper
Salt

1. Dissolve the chicken base in the water in a heavy pot.

2. Boil the zucchini, onions, celery, and garlic in this liquid until tender and then puree.

3. Return the puree to the pot and add the heavy cream and the whole cream.

4. Stir in the cornstarch to thicken and heat well, but not to boiling. Season with curry powder, white pepper, and salt. Garnish with a slice of lemon, sprig of fresh dill, and an artfully added sprinkle of cayenne pepper.

New York–born John Quitman wrote of Natchez, "It is…a charming life [where] one quits thinking and takes to dreaming." Today his home, Monmouth, embodies the very best of Southern hospitality.

Leave Route 5 (the highway that runs between Richmond and Williamsburg), wind along a twisting rural Charles City, Virginia "black top," turn onto the dirt road, and in the midst of rich farmland is North Bend.

North Bend

No matter how diligently we tried, most days Walter and I ran late. By nightfall we'd look at one another and laughingly chant the old cliché, "Time flies when you're having fun," while trying to figure out how to explain our tardiness to the next appointment—some exasperated person who, by now, was wondering if we'd even show. Thursday, August 19, was no different.

By the time we arrived at North Bend, it was way past 10 P.M. Now, that doesn't sound late to the sophisticated city diner who prefers a 9 P.M. seating. But to the farmer who rises to greet the sun, these are sleeping, not waking, hours. A farmer's wife, Ridgely Copland, lost little time letting us know we were late—very, very late—when we finally arrived at North Bend, a rambling, 1819 white frame farmhouse with red roof, set in the middle of corn and soybean fields at the end of a dirt road off Virginia Route 5.

"You'll have to excuse me if I'm not at my best," she apologized sleepily. "I dozed off waiting for you. I go to work at seven-fifteen. But," she added, "let me show you around first. I won't be here in the morning. George will get your breakfast. George," she half called, half yawned down the long hall, "Daddy, they're here."

We were anything *but* sleepy. After our frenzied daytime pace, we need wind-down time at night. That's when we become, according to Walter, "wired."

After our usual apologies and fumbled excuses, we began lugging my suitcase, Attila, and Walter's overstuffed canvas camera bags toward the back stairs, when Ridgely suddenly stopped us.

"Wait. See that picture?" she asked, pointing our attention to a family portrait. "It's the eyebrows," she said in a more wide-awake, cheerful voice. "George has those eyebrows." I looked. They were Abe Lincoln eyebrows, I thought. Not sure what ire my Yankee reference might provoke, I kept silent.

George, Ridgely's husband, and the great-great-nephew of Sarah Harrison, the original owner of North Bend, does have bushy eyebrows, twinkling eyes, and a farmer's hands. He also cooks up the best, crispiest waffles and fattest slabs of country ham within miles. George joined us and in no time everyone forgot the late hour.

We toured the house, learned about its past, and, best of all, Walter and I got to know gentle, folksy Ridgely and George Copland so well that we plopped down in their comfortable kitchen and talked far into the morning hours.

We talked about simple things in that homey setting—the land, farming, the usual

Thomas Jefferson, Virginia statesman, gentleman, farmer— and friend of George Copland's ancestors—wrote, "Let the farmer forevermore be honored in his calling, for they who labor in the earth are the chosen people of God." Here, in their kitchen, complete with George's daybed for a nap after long hours in the fields, are the folksy Coplands and Muriel Crump.

August drought, the garden, family china, and old things. We learned about Civil War battles fought nearby and Sheridan's encampment on those very grounds. We heard about the people who visit North Bend from afar, the neighboring plantation houses, President William Henry Harrison (George's great-great uncle), and the old days.

When we finally wound down for the night, I was ready for the big, inviting brass bed piled with fluffed-up pillows that awaited. I dashed to the bathroom only to discover I had two tubes of toothpaste but no toothbrush with me.

I muttered something about "If this were a Marriott Courtyard [where Walter and I always stay when not at a historic resting place], I could go down to the desk at any hour and get one." Then I remembered that George

Washington had worn wooden false teeth and I laughingly told myself, "It's not that bad. Just make do until we pass a convenience store on our way to Richmond."

But as I crawled into bed, my humor and good spirits faded. I was filled with loneliness.

You see, everyone I meet on my wonderful journeys to write these books invariably says, "You lead the most exciting, glamorous life, *and* you love what you do!"

They're right. But people forget that everyone has grief and pain, and at that point in my life, I was very low. If Shakespeare's King Richard III had the winter of his discontent, this was the summer of my gloom.

My octogenarian parents were wracked with one major health problem after the other. My thirty-year marriage had ended in divorce, and I was nursing a broken heart from a dream-come-true romance gone bad that I couldn't get over.

No matter how exhilarating and interesting my days with Walter were, my nightmare nights were filled with despair. Sleep, when it came, was for only two, three, four hours. Even in summer days of early light, I awakened in morning darkness.

That night, though, my loneliness was less pervasive. My spirits had been lifted by the warm, unassuming way the Coplands had made us feel at home, despite the inconvenience our late arrival had caused. Eventually I drifted off to sleep.

⌣

The country sun filtering through an uninterrupted open sky is clearer, even on hazy days, than the city sun blocked by buildings and smog. The country air, even on humid days, fresher. And the birds sing.

I awakened to a bobwhite's song. The sun streamed through the nineteenth-century wavy-glass panes. I hadn't slept so well or so

Homemade syrups and preserves are the order of the day at North Bend—all served in family pieces. I had tea served from this charming rosebud-decorated teapot— one that George's mother kept hot on the woodstove. The marks on the bottom remain to this day.

long since May. My nose told me breakfast was ready. I bounded into the bathroom. The shower stall was roomy and modern, but the lukewarm water only trickled down. It didn't seem to matter. But I desperately wanted a toothbrush. I put an ample squirt of gel on my finger, stuck it in my mouth, and began scrubbing.

Then I realized the mirror was the door of a medicine cabinet. I opened it. There was everything a forgetful traveler needed—fold-up toothbrushes, little soaps, disposable razors, toothpaste—and I didn't even have to go down to the front desk, or call housekeeping.

"You look ten years younger," Walter told me as I wolfed down the second waffle that George offered me.

These weren't waffles that had sat out and cooled down on the table. Our host and cook brought them in hot, fresh off the griddle. As I smothered mine with melted butter served in a Blue Willow pitcher and Ridgely's homemade cherry syrup, I was reminded of Henry Barnard's account of a breakfast he had eaten in 1833 at a nearby Virginia plantation where he was served "hot muffins and corn batter cakes every 2 minutes."

But our breakfast treat was only beginning. Ridgely had played hookey and stayed home from work that day.

"George may be the descendant, but he's really more interested in farming than he is the history. I thought I ought to be here to tell you about the family and the furniture and all," she said mischievously. (I did notice that she didn't offer to help with the cooking, though.)

Soon joining us at the table were other North Bend guests, Alain and Monique Conqe, and their exquisite sixteen-year-old daughter, Marie, tourists from Paris. Alain, we learned, is a political journalist.

Between Walter's fractured French, Alain's slow English, Monique's bilingual translations, my effusive hand gestures, Marie's shy, amused looks, George's delicious breakfast, and Ridgely's fresh smiles, we managed to cover topics from the Bosnian conflict to where the Conqes' travels should take them next. We rerouted them to Nags Head and Charlottesville so that by the time they got back to D.C. to catch their plane the next week, they would have a spare day to attend a dinner party in their honor at Walter's Washington home.

I, meanwhile, was in my element.

"Don't you see? This is a picture of the olden days!" My words came tumbling out. "Here we are, strangers, Southerners and foreigners alike—and the French loved the South," I pointedly added. "Here we are finding common bonds around a beautiful banquet-size plantation table that is overflowing with bountiful food. We're talking, we're laughing, we're exchanging views, we're making new friends—why, we even have an invitation to dinner a week away and a hundred miles from here. In a word, this is the *essence* of Southern hospitality—this is *sharing*. The only difference is that it's the 1990s, not the 1790s!"

Now, if my enthusiasm sounds excessive, I ask you to follow my thoughts along with me.

This house, North Bend, built in 1819, was sold in 1844 by Sarah Harrison to Thomas Willcox. Through industry and insight, by 1853 he had doubled the property in size and productivity. Nine short years later, in 1864, with the invasion of 30,000 Union

troops, Willcox was forced out of his home. General Philip Sheridan claimed the house as his Union headquarters.

Land that once yielded food and sustenance became a battleground, littered with broken bodies and shattered dreams. Rooms that once resounded with laughter became a warring place, littered with battle maps, plots to kill and destroy.

Those war years brought unbearable sadness to the Southern people and the homes and land they loved so much. In 1865 Willcox sold the property, never to return to his land, his home. Yet here we were with Sarah's descendants, 130 years later.

Once again the land is productive, the rooms filled with laughter and hope. North Bend, once again, is a loving home, lived in by a kind family that gives its best to others—even down to a make-do toothbrush.

I took a heavy heart with me to North Bend. It was not mended when I left, but it was much lighter. That is the unspoken, healing gift of Southern hospitality.

The family's walnut plantation desk where, in 1945, the original map General Sheridan used to overtake this very land was found hidden in a secret compartment.

In the rolling hills outside of Brenham, Texas, Jane and John Barnhill have transformed a rare and treasured nineteenth-century homestead found in ruins into a disarmingly charming cabin and preserved it for generations to come.

Living the Book I'm Writing

~

"How do you find these wonderful places?" my North Carolina–born but now Denver-till-he-dies cousin, Arnold Joslin, asked.

"I pick up the phone and start calling around," I explained. "I tell everyone that I'm writing a book on Southern hospitality and things fall into place. You wouldn't believe how helpful people are."

"Sounds to me like you're living the book you're writing." Arnold smiled.

He was right. And nowhere did I live that generous, helpful, Southern hospitality more fully than on my jaunt to eastern Texas.

It started when Amy Hendrix answered my blind phone call to the corporate head-quarters of Blue Bell Creameries, a world-class and world-famous ice creamery in little Brenham, Texas. Half an hour later I was stunned to get a call from Jane Barnhill, wife of one of Blue Bell's vice presidents!

She began by saying "We're thrilled you're coming here. What may I do to help you?"

"I need to find a country fair, a rodeo, a Texas dance, the best barbecue around, and, oh yes . . . a place to stay—something uniquely Texas," I reeled off spit-fire fast.

"Let's start with the last one. How does an 1850s log house built by one of the 'Old Three Hundred' settlers sound? Now, Tex's Bar-B-Que is open on Thursday through Sunday. What days will you be here? I'll have to look into finding a fair for you . . . and a rodeo . . . and a dance," she drawled in her charming, ladylike Texas voice. "When can I call you back?"

Jane Barnhill, as I learned during our many phone conversations, not only is well-known for her historic preservation efforts, she's also a full-time grandmother (though she looks more like a model than she does anyone's granny) plus the organist and youth choir director for the Presbyterian Church.

And, once we met face to face, as always happens in the South, it turns out that she's the friend of several friends of mine.

It was well after midnight when Walter and I pulled off the gravel road and drove up to the James Walker Homestead, the 1850s log house once used as a barn but now an elegantly rustic bed and breakfast cottage. A bottle of wine, cheese and crackers, a year's supply of Blue Bell ice cream, and a welcoming note awaited us.

If I'd known the beauty of the landscape I'd see the next morning, I would have stayed up to watch the sun rise. Instead I was awakened when Walter opened the kitchen door and I heard the deep, soft mooing of a cow.

"Is that sound effects or what?" I called out as I reluctantly opened one eye. There, through the open-shuttered window of my room, I beheld the prettiest Texas pasture you can imagine. It looked more like a lush English landscape painted by Gainsborough than a scene from real life.

The golden sun in the bluebonnet-blue Texas sky swept across the green hills and rolling earth, casting a mellow, early-morning glow on all below. In the far distance a red-brown cow stood frozen in time beside a crystal-clear pond. Nearer the house the undulating earth rose and fell, dotted here and there with clumps of leafy oak trees.

Only when I heard a mockingbird's song coming from the crepe myrtle branches by the back porch did I know I was looking at God's great out-of-doors and not a painted canvas.

This is a part of Texas I had not seen before. I knew some of the cities firsthand, big ones like Houston and Dallas, and some of the good-size ones like Lubbock and Beaumont.

I had driven hundreds of miles across the Texas interstates.

But I had never breathed *this* Texas air nor seen *this* Texas beauty. The air and the earth wrapped itself around me. No wonder the people from Virginia and Georgia loved the land and settled there. It reminded them of home.

Our two and a half days in Brenham, that twelve-thousand-person hamlet chock full of antique shops, turn-of-the-century houses, Blue Bell ice cream, roses and black-eyed Susans, pit-cooked barbecue, always smiling, helpful, hospitable people, and beautiful countryside, were too short—especially at dusk and at dawn when the sun set and rose as if to give us "Southerners from up East" a special Texas show.

"You know what, Walter?" I asked as he slammed down the trunk and we pulled out of the driveway to head back to New Orleans. "I think I could live here."

Wouldn't you know that Texas cows give the best cream? Ask anyone who's ever tasted Blue Bell ice cream. It's been made in Brenham since 1911 and is famous world-round.

A Special Recipe from Richmond Hill

John Babb, Richmond Hill's executive chef, says he's just giving a "Southern accent" to his dishes when he adds traditional Southern touches to a time-tested international recipe. We said the Southern gods had kissed his creations. It was hard to choose a single recipe from all the delicious dishes, but I finally decided upon this one.

MOUNTAIN APPLE AND VIDALIA ONION SOUP

Serves 12

6 quarts beef stock
2 quarts apple cider
3 bay leaves
1 tablespoon thyme leaves
2 tablespoons coarse ground black pepper
1 tablespoon salt
6 pounds thinly sliced Vidalia onion
12 tablespoons butter
1 tablespoon sugar
2 cups dry sherry

GARNISH

Aged Gruyère cheese
Parmesan cheese
Garlic croutons
4 cups North Carolina red apples, diced and chilled, held in cider

1. Place beef stock and apple cider in large soup pot. Bring to a light boil. Add the bay leaves, thyme, black pepper, and salt. Let simmer for 1 hour.

2. Sauté onions with butter; after onions are partially cooked, add salt and sugar. (The sugar helps the onions to brown.) After the onions are browned and thoroughly done, deglaze the pan with sherry and add to the beef and cider stock. Simmer for 1 hour.

3. To serve, ladle soup into soup crocks and top with garlic croutons, floating on top of soup, then top with Parmesan and Gruyère. Brown under broiler for 1 to 2 minutes. Top with diced apples just before serving.

There's a secret to gaining the most from a stay at Richmond Hill above the French Broad River in Asheville, North Carolina (opposite and right). After breakfast, before setting off on that day's travel, take the time to enjoy a leisurely rocking spell on the front porch. You'll add hours to your night's rest as you breathe in the serenity of the Southern landscape.

Eating My Way Through the South

I won't see anybody I know, I rationalized as I dashed into Harris Teeter to pick up a few groceries for supper. Dressed in summer gardening grubbies (T-shirt, shorts, socks, and tennis shoes), my hair uncombed, and with glasses on, I was sure no one would recognize me anyway. ∼ I was wheeling the grocery cart from aisle to aisle in my hurry-up New York City way when I heard the dreaded words. ∼ "Mary Louise? Mary Louise!" ∼ I stopped dead in my tracks. ∼ Garrison Keillor once said that some people won't go back to their hometowns because their friends will call them by their old nick-

A plate piled high with Southern delicacies calls for ample helpings of homemade pickles and relishes.

names— in the South names like Butch, Sis, Bubba.

When I'm in Danville, my hometown, people call me by my *real* name, Mary Louise. (Let me explain my new name. You take the "M" from Mary, the "L" from Louise, and you put them together, "M.L.," but you spell out, Emyl. My Yankee college roommate, Susy Thurber, gave me that distinctive nickname, but that's another story. Mary Louise is what people in Danville call me.)

"Yes, ma'am?" (That's how people in Danville, even fifty-year-olds, respond to our mother's friends whose names we can't remember.)

"How's your cookbook coming? Have you finished it yet?" Mother's friend asked me enthusiastically.

I drew myself up to my full "author" status.

"It's *not* a cookbook," I replied somewhat haughtily. "It's a book about Southern *hospitality*."

"Oh." My mother's friend's face fell.

"When you spoke to the Wednesday Club (Wednesday's the day the women's club meets in Danville) you said you were writing a cookbook next."

"No," I emphatically corrected her, "I said I was going to *eat* my way through the South."

"Well, I was going to send you my Sally Lunn recipe," she said sweetly, but obviously disappointed.

I felt terrible. Here was wonderful Southern hospitality—sharing your best with others—being extended to me at 3 P.M. in the middle of the grocery store on a hot summer's day and in my impatience and frustration I had forgotten my Southern manners.

Furthermore Virginians are proud of their culinary heritage. America's first published cookbook, *The Virginia Housewife, or Methodical Cook*, was written by a Virginian, Mary Randolph. Her work was so highly thought of that Susan Dabney Smedes wrote that George Orris, the butler at Elmington, a flourishing Virginia plantation, "was said to know by heart every recipe in Mrs. Randolph's cookery-book, having been trained by that lady herself." But then she adds, "Virginia tradition says that Mrs. Randolph had spent three fortunes in cooking!" To write a cookbook would be in a noble Virginia tradition.

"Oh, I'd love to have it," I said, my voice full of apologies. But I must sadly report, she never sent it. Maybe she will if she reads this.

Never fear though. Another Sally Lunn recipe *is* included in this chapter—a chapter of Southern recipes—my gift to you of the best others have given to me. Here is a sampler of some of the delicious Southern fare we tasted as Walter and I literally did eat our way through the South.

The truth is, the more we tasted, the more

I wanted to write a cookbook—not just to compile delectable and distinctive recipes, but to gather enjoyable stories, savor stimulating conversation, and store away wonderful memories. Louise Hale said it best in her 1916 book, *We Discover the Old Dominion*: "A circle of chairs is never provocative of good talk unless there is a table in the middle. In France when conversation was even more of an art than it is now they never rose at the end of a meal fearing to break the flow of thought with the flow of bowl."

Walter and I will more than willingly blame our late-night hours and the extra pounds we each gained along the way on the wonderful food that made the conversation flow so easily day after day!

I first became aware of the pleasures *and* the conviviality of eating out when I was no more than four or five years old and growing up in Robbins, North Carolina.

Spivey's was the town's restaurant, and everyone ate there—mill superintendents, farmers in overalls, the Baptist minister in his red tie, mill workers, everyone. The booths and tables held no more than fifteen or twenty people, but then Robbins only had four or five hundred residents.

Its one room was always full, but none of us remembers ever waiting to be seated. Maybe that's because, like small-town Southern churches, this was where you saw your friends and had a good time. We went on Friday nights and feasted on fried oysters (my father still insists that they were the best he ever had anywhere), country-fried steak, and fried chicken. In a word, I looked forward to Friday nights all week long.

Sundays were quite different. We had to drive twenty-five miles to Southern Pines to attend the Episcopal church services. Mother said it would take too long to cook a full meal after we got home, so we ate most Sunday dinners (as they were called) either in Southern Pines or Pinehurst.

Unlike Spivey's in Robbins, these Southern resort restaurants were quietly elegant. I don't remember what we ate, but I do remember how grand the ladies and gentlemen eating there looked.

Granny's china, old-time recipes— the makings of Southern meals.

I also remember the food, the company and the conversation on those Sundays when we were invited to the Busbees' log cabin in Jugtown. Those meals and visits were like no others then or now.

Despite their rustic home, Jacques and Juliana Busbee were not country people. They were artists in the fullest sense—educated, sophisticated bohemians. The Busbees' lifelong endeavor was to keep alive North Carolina's folk crafts. In Moore County they found that the potter's art was living but languishing.

They took the best pottery they could find to New York, where people were charmed by its naive forms and beautiful glazes. In the late 1910s Mrs. Busbee opened a tearoom in the basement of an old house at Washington Square in Greenwich Village, and soon "Jugtown Pottery" was known worldwide.

When we moved to Robbins in 1946 the Busbees had retired to their secluded North Carolina home where, nonetheless, travelers came to see and buy Jugtown Pottery. Mother's and the Busbees' families had been friends for generations, so we were often guests for Sunday dinner.

Although the Busbees were dedicated to their mission, they clearly missed city life. They raised vegetables and lived "off the earth," but Mrs. Busbee was no country girl. I remember eating squash and tomatoes and peas that looked and tasted unlike any others I had seen up to that time for Mrs. Busbee prepared exotic, ethnic dishes. I had a lot of time to study the food on my plate because I was never included in the conversation, which centered around Washington politics, postwar Europe, art, philosophy, and music.

After a seemingly endless dinner hour (for me), Mrs. Busbee momentarily disappeared to the kitchen and returned with a punch-bowl–size Jugtown bowl filled with soapy water. She then proceeded to wash the dishes so she would not miss a word of conversation, nor, I would add, the chance to voice her opinion!

I have remembered her custom many times when I have slipped into the kitchen, only to hear the chatter and laughter of my own dinner guests through the closed door, and wondered What am I missing? In fact, it is said that Southern hostesses serve con-

A visit to Columbus, Georgia, sets the record straight. Coca-Cola was founded here by Dr. John Pemberton—not in Atlanta.

gealed salads and casseroles so they won't have to spend valuable guest time in the kitchen.

Yes, food brings out the best in all of us. As the great literary gourmet M. F. K. Fisher wrote, mankind has a "fundamental need to celebrate the high points of his life by eating and drinking."

Walter and I found our Southern hospitality adventure full of high points, so many, in fact, that there were times when we rivaled the gastronomic schedule that Major-General Chevalier de Chastellus described in his account of his Virginia travels in 1780. He had "An excellent breakfast at nine o'clock, a sumptuous dinner at two, tea and punch in the afternoon, and an elegant little supper divided the day most happily for those whose stomaches were never unprepared."

Like my earliest dining-out experiences in Robbins, here is a smorgasbord of recipes— a mixture of homestyle dishes and elegant cuisine. Just remember Letitia Burwell's mid-nineteenth–century sound advice: "Have no shams. Procure an abundance of the freshest, richest, real cream, milk, eggs, butter, lard, best old Madeira wine, all the way from Madeira."

⌐⌐

"Every Virginia housewife knew how to compound all the various dishes in Mrs. Randolph's cookery book, and our tables were filled with every species of meat and vegetable to be found on a plantation, with every kind of cakes, jellies, and blanc-mange to be concocted out of eggs, butter, and cream, besides an endless catalogue of preserves, sweetmeats, pickles and condiments."
Letitia M. Burwell

Signs of Down Home Hospitality

Forget the tablecloths. Nothing beats the down-home fun and flavor of all manners of Southern country cooking.

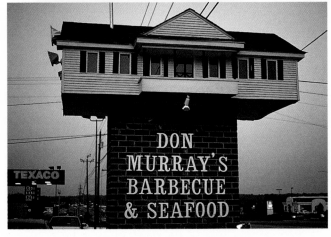

SALLY LUNN

Makes 1 loaf

Sally Lunn is such a long-standing favorite at my Southern mother's home that when Joslin was a little girl she affectionately called her granny's Sally Lunn "Granny Lunn." The slightly sweet bread is delicious cut, buttered, and toasted for breakfast. It is also the perfect accompaniment for dishes that call for a toast base.

It's appropriate that this Sally Lunn recipe comes from Vivian Greene, a chef at Indian Fields, a popular restaurant on Route 5, Virginia, better known as the James River Plantation Road. Sally Lunn has been a staple in Virginia homes since the eighteenth century.

⅔ cake yeast
¼ cup melted butter
2 cups milk, warmed
6 cups all-purpose flour
1 tablespoon salt
¾ cup sugar
6 eggs

1. Dissolve the yeast into butter and milk.

2. In a large bowl, mix all the dry ingredients for 5 minutes. Add the milk and butter mix. Let the mixture sit for 10 minutes.

3. Start the mixer and let the dough come together. Add the eggs one at a time until they are completely incorporated.

4. Stop the mixer and cover the dough. Let it rise in a warm place until double in size (about 30 to 45 minutes).

5. After the dough has risen, knead it with the mixer for 1 to 2 minutes.

6. Portion the dough into 4 well-greased loaf pans and cover. Let the dough rise until it reaches the top of the pan.

7. Bake in a preheated 375° F. oven for 25 minutes.

KENTUCKY BEATEN BISCUITS

*Makes about 1½ to 2 dozen
2-inch biscuits*

When Sara Hicks, an eighteen-year-old bride from upstate New York, wrote home to her parents in 1853 from her husband's North Carolina plantation, she described biscuits made "with shortening and without anything to make them light and beaten like crackers." These days Southerners *still* talk about beaten biscuits—those their grandmothers used to make—but few have the stamina to undertake the task themselves. Who, after all, wants to follow a recipe that calls for "one quart of flour, lard the size of a hen's egg, one teaspoonful of salt" and instructs the cook to beat this concoction for an hour?

But once upon a time, in those days before the feminist movement, beaten biscuits were even credited with holding a marriage together. Marjorie Kinnan Rawlings, in her classic book, *Cross Creek Cookery*, tells of her Northern friend who refused to bother with "the hours-long trouble" it took to make this Southern delicacy for her Kentucky husband. "Just as the marriage was about to go on the rocks, and rightly, she saw the light," Rawlings wrote. "Beaten biscuits now hold the happy household together."

The tradition of Kentucky beaten biscuits remains so strong that every four years, on

There are those occasions when only etched crystal, French lace tablecloths, English bone china, sterling silver, and of course, freshly gathered Southern garden flowers, will do. Pebble Hill, Thomasville, Georgia.

inauguration morning, the state's newly elected governor is treated to an 8 A.M. breakfast of beaten biscuits, country ham, fruit, and Lane Cake (a rich cake with a coconut, raisin, and nut filling) made by neighborhood ladies in Frankfort. Their beaten biscuit recipe is a time-honored one, but the nineteenth-century beaten biscuit machine helps speed up the process. And it certainly is much more civilized than using a baseball bat like one friend of mine's grandmother used to do!

If you're not familiar with beaten biscuits, you may not like them. They are not 2 inches high, nor have they a flakey outside. Someone once described them as a cross between a fallen biscuit and a saltine cracker. Actually, they are rather similar to an unleavened bread, in other words, bland, but to those who love them, there's no substitute for the beaten biscuit—especially with real Southern country ham.

For the taste and the texture, that unmistakable combination of a hard outside and tender inside, try this updated version from John Egerton, the author of *Southern Food at Home, on the Road, in History*—a grand book.

To John's recipe, I must add that all authentic beaten biscuits *must* have pricked tops. Some people prefer three rows of pricking, while others insist upon four. It sounds as if these pricks are for aesthetic reasons but, because the dough has been "beaten" so thoroughly, the pricks are needed to release the air between the many thin layers of dough that will expand when cooking.

When making the pricks, be sure your fork pierces all the layers and goes through the biscuit. You may want to check the bottom of the first few biscuits you prick to make sure you're doing it correctly.

2 cups all-purpose flour
¼ teaspoon salt
¼ teaspoon baking powder
1 tablespoon sugar
¼ cup lard
⅓ cup milk or half-and-half

1. Preheat the oven to 325°F.

2. Combine the flour, salt, baking powder, and sugar. Sift together 3 times.

3. Cut in the lard using a pastry blender. Add the milk (or half-and-half) and knead into a firm ball. If more liquid is needed, add it a teaspoon at a time, taking care not to get the dough too moist.

4. Break the dough ball into pieces and put all of it in a food processor to spin with the dough blade for 2 minutes. Remove the dough and knead it a few minutes. Then roll and fold the dough by hand several times.

5. When it becomes smooth, roll the dough to ¼-inch thickness. Cut the biscuits with a biscuit cutter, pierce each one with a fork, and bake for 30 minutes, or until they are slightly browned on the bottom and a smooth, pale tan on top. Leave them in the oven with the heat off for a few more minutes.

My Kentucky friend Gene Burch captured these action shots of beating the biscuits for Governor Brereton Jones' Inauguration Day breakfast in 1992. This only happens once every four years!

BOUDIN BALLS

Makes about 35 to 40 balls

I've always had an aversion for recipes with the directions "Form into a ball. Roll in crumbs. Dip in slightly beaten egg. Roll again in crumbs. Fry in deep, hot fat until brown."

When I was growing up, chicken croquettes swimming in a cream sauce with little green peas were a weekly staple. To my young eyes they looked as bad as they tasted. When I saw "boudin balls" on the menu at the St. Francisville Inn in Lousiana I didn't know they would be rolled in crumbs and fat fried or, in other words, be "croquettes," but they are.

Ken Sansone, the art director at Crown Publishers who was along on this trip, first asked about the "bou*dan*" balls, in his strong New York voice.

"Those are *beau*d'n balls," our waitress sweetly corrected him. Who could pass up a dish that sounded so different, so Southern?

As I bit one, I remembered Marjorie Kinnan Rawlings' comment about grits, raw onion, and sardine dish. She said, "I tasted dubiously, and remained to gorge."

These croquettes are scrumptious—not at all like those oversize, lightly soggy "mystery mounds" of my childhood. When these distinctly Southern appetizers are served with a slightly sweet honey-mustard sauce for dipping, the combination of their meaty flavor and crunchy texture with the light sauce is memorable. You'll want to gorge.

2½ pounds lean pork
½ pound calf's liver
2 cups seasoned stock
½ cup chopped green onions
1 cup chopped fresh parsley
¾ cup chopped green pepper
1 tablespoon chopped garlic
1 tablespoon chopped dried sage leaves
1 tablespoon cayenne pepper
1 teaspoon black pepper
2½ cups cooked rice
Seasoned flour
Oil for deep-frying

1. In a large skillet, cover the pork and liver with the stock. Bring to a boil over high heat. Skim off the foam. Reduce the heat and simmer for an hour. Spoon out the meat. Discard the liquid.

2. In a food processer, grind the meat to medium. In a large bowl, combine the chopped meat and the remaining ingredients except the seasoned flour and oil. Mix well. Knead the mixture until it sticks together. Form 2-inch balls, and coat with seasoned flour. (I do this by putting flour in a bag and adding a handful of the balls at a time. When each is well coated, remove the balls. Repeat until all are coated.) Deep-fry at 350 degrees, or cook them like meatballs in a skillet.

3. Serve with honey-creole mustard or a similar sauce. Honey-creole mustard can be ordered from Bayou Sara (see page 190).

There's a bountiful plenty to give thanks for at Mrs. Wilkes' in Savannah. Guests sit down to twelve different vegetables and six meat dishes. But the house dessert remains the same— banana pudding.

Breakfast at Eight

At eight o'clock you take your seat at the breakfast table of rich mahogany, each plate standing separate on its own little cloth. Mr. Carter will sit at one end of the table and Mrs. Carter at the other. . . . Mr. Carter has a cold ham before him of the real Virginia flavor; this is all the meat you get in the morning, but the servant will bring you hot muffins and corn batter cakes . . . you will find on the table also loaf wheat books, hot and cold corn bread.

Henry Bernard describing breakfast at Shirley Plantation, Virginia, in 1833

At Maymont in Richmond, Virginia, heirloom Haviland fish and game china are displayed in a monumental rose-wood cabinet shown at the 1855 Paris Exposition Universalle. These objects belonged to James and Sallie Mae Dooley who bequeathed their palatial home and gardens to the citizens of Richmond as a public park and museum.

Anyone who can sit down at a beautifully appointed breakfast table and eat only cereal need not travel through the South. Part of "diving right in" and tasting the joy and conviviality of Southern hospitality begins with savoring the flavors of a plantation-style breakfast. At a bed and breakfast the experience is heightened by the conversation with the hosts and other guests. But sometimes it is also pleasant to steal quiet time and be served in your room. It's the same way at home. Sometimes we want family and friends around. Other mornings you're your own best friend.

That's what I found one late-spring morning at Graylyn, the grand family home of the Grays of Winston-Salem, North Carolina. A 1920s mansion that combines the best of French and English architecture with the lovely rolling hills of western North Carolina, Graylyn has a unique distinction: It is a state-of-the-art conference center for Wake Forest University that has been showered with awards and highest honors. It is also the place where Oprah Winfrey chose to honor one of our nation's great poets, North Carolinian Maya Angelou, with a celebrity party that made headline news.

From Graylyn's kitchen, here is a scrumptious breakfast dish you should not miss. Remember, even if you're not a "breakfast person," there's always brunch.

GRAYLYN'S EGGS SARDU

Serves 1 (prepare as many Sardu as people present)

1 English muffin
1 large egg
2–3 leaves fresh spinach
1 tablespoon butter
2 artichoke hearts, canned
Salt and pepper

1. Split and toast the English muffin until golden.

2. Poach the egg in an egg poacher for 4 to 5 minutes.

3. Wilt the spinach in a sauté pan with the butter. Remove and drain it on a clean dry towel.

4. Add the artichoke hearts to the same pan. Season with salt and pepper and cook until warmed through.

5. Place the spinach on top of the English muffin and top off with the egg and artichoke hearts.

6. Cover with Hollandaise sauce. (Recipe follows.)

The best company for a morning meal alone is often a good book. Here, for your enjoyment is food for thought from We Discover the Old Dominion, written in 1916 by Louise Closser Hale. "To the South [colonists] brought the customs of England, indeed are clinging to them now. In New England they abandoned all hint of court life as quickly as possible. It may have been the influence of climate for the settlements of both localities endured through incredible hardships. But I should like to have seen how the Puritans would have disported themselves had they gone to the lotus-eating country instead of a land with a diet of rocks."

HOLLANDAISE SAUCE

3 medium egg yolks
1 tablespoon water
1 teaspoon lemon juice
1 teaspoon salt
2 cups clarified butter
Dash cayenne pepper

1. Bring water in the bottom of a double boiler to a rolling boil.

2. Combine all the ingredients except the butter and cayenne in the top of the double boiler and place it over the boiling water.

3. Whip the egg mixture constantly until it is lemon colored and forms ribbons.

4. Remove the pot from the heat and add the melted butter in a slow stream, whipping the mixture to combine. Add a dash of cayenne and pour over Sardu.

At Uglesich's I am told that the freshest, plumpest oysters are those off the boats at Borgne. With a little luck, you might even find a pearl or two in your dozen.

Oysters and Other Seafood Delights

"I remember an oyster supper given by my father, the bivalves being eaten raw or roasted in their shells. Uncle William Plummer offered me one raw, but it was offensive to my taste. He endeavored to induce me to swallow it by the offer of a nine-pence (12½ cents). I made faithful efforts but failed. I then had a settled belief that I could not eat oysters, but eighteen years later, I was detained in court until after the dinner-hour. The only food left at the hotel table was oyster-pie. Urged by extreme hunger, I was tempted to eat some. I never tasted anything so exquisite. Ever since then I find oysters in any shape palatable."
Kemp Plummer Battle,
Memories of an Old-Time Tar Heel

∿

No Southern journal or memories, to say nothing of cookbook—from John Smith's Jamestown days to the present—is complete without some praise of the oyster. For those who love plump, juicy oysters, a trip to Uglesich's is worth the cost of the airfare to New Orleans.

Now, Uglesich's is not for the faint-hearted. It is a luncheonette in the old sense of the word. No fancy "oyster bar" nomenclature for Gail and Anthony Uglesich. They've been in the same somewhat seedy location since 1927. That's three years after Anthony's father began his restaurant on Rampart Street. Emily, Anthony's mother, still helps out, even though her ninetieth birthday is creeping up.

When I went there for the first time, I might have kept going right past the barred-up windows if I hadn't realized my rented car would be safe parked next to the Jaguars and Mercedes in the narrow parking strip at the side of the building.

And I might not have waited for the hour and a half that I did if Emeril, one of New Orleans' most highly acclaimed chefs, had not told me the night before that he eats lunch there any chance he gets.

Don't expect anything other than the best food you can imagine and the friendliest true New Orleans atmosphere you can find in the entire city. Overlook the crumbs on the table and don't worry about the homeless regular who wanders in the back door looking for a handout. Anthony Uglesich will see to it that he gets fed, and in return, he'll soon sweep up. Anthony wouldn't tell you this himself, but I've stuck around Uglesich's quite a few times now and I'll wager that a hefty part of his day's cash sales go out the door in charity food gifts. That's the warm-hearted sort of guy he is.

His help never leaves him. I see the same always-grinning smiles every time I'm there.

And then there's George—an Uglesich institution. He had delivered bread to them for thirty-two years, and when he retired he dropped by one day, out of habit, I guess. He's been there ever since—serving and singing to country music tapes.

You can't buy Uglesich's atmosphere. You couldn't put together such a cast of naturals if you tried. But don't be misled. You'll pay New Orleans prices for your soft-shell crabs (the best I have ever put in my mouth) or whatever your pleasure might be—but you're still getting the best buy in town.

The old standards are always on the menu, but Anthony has to keep his health-conscious regulars happy—the doctors and judges and businessmen who can't stay away—so he happily tries out new treats to satisfy them. He's gotten so he regularly uses many of today's new products, like those in his seafood-stuffed pasta recipe that he shared with me.

I've had it. It's delicious. It's made with healthy ingredients. It's quite simple and I recommend it.

Still these days I get to New Orleans quite frequently and take friends who have never been there to Uglesich's for lunch. After a half-dozen oysters fresh in from the boats at Borgne, I have a soft-shell crab—or two.

I don't know where the temptations and indulgences are greater—on board the Mississippi Queen, or on shore at the restaurants found in the many ports of call that stretch along this great river.

EGGPLANT WITH SHRIMP AND OYSTER SAUCE

Serves 6

Not everyone likes raw oysters, but many enjoy an occasional taste of plump, succulent cooked oysters. This appetizer is from Susiana, one of the antebellum bed and breakfasts we visited that serves marvelous dinners as well. This recipe can also be used as a luncheon or even light supper dish.

Walter liked it so much that he ate his at our elegant candlelight dinner, and the next morning, after Anne-Marie cooked up a fresh order for us to photograph in the daylight, he ate it, before breakfast!

SHRIMP MIXTURE
¼ cup (½ stick) unsalted butter
½ onion, chopped
1 teaspoon salt
1 teaspoon black pepper
½ teaspoon cayenne pepper
1 teaspoon thyme
3 stalks celery, chopped
1 green pepper, chopped
7–8 shrimp per person, peeled and deveined

1. In a large skillet, sauté the onion in the butter. Stir in the salt, peppers, thyme, celery, and green peppers. Add 7 or 8 shrimp per person and stir until the shrimp turn pink.

EGGPLANT SLICES
6 slices eggplant
Flour for dredging
1 beaten egg
Plain bread crumbs

Peel and soak 6 slices of eggplant in salted water for a few minutes. Drain the eggplant, dip it in flour, beaten egg, and bread crumbs. Fry on both sides in heated oil.

OYSTER SAUCE
¼ cup (½) stick unsalted butter
½ onion, chopped
1 clove garlic, chopped
½ teaspoon salt
½ teaspoon black pepper
½ teaspoon ground nutmeg
2 tablespoons all-purpose flour
1 cup heavy cream
½ pint oysters with juice
½ fresh lemon

1. Melt the butter in a large skillet. Add the onion and garlic sauté until transparent, 5 to 7 minutes. Stir in the salt, pepper, nutmeg, and flour.

2. Make into a smooth paste and stir in the cream. Cook slowly, stirring constantly, until thickened.

3. Add the oysters and their juice along with the juice of ½ lemon. Cook until the oysters plump up, about 5 minutes.

4. To serve, heap a portion of the shrimp mixture onto an eggplant slice and a portion of the oysters and sauce around the eggplant.

RUTLEDGE HOUSE INN'S SHE-CRAB SOUP

~

Serves 4-6

One of the South's signature recipes originated quite by accident, once again giving credence to the maxim—Necessity is the mother of invention. While preparing for a formal dinner given by Charleston's mayor, the butler of the house was asked to liven up the rather bland cream soup. Sweet orange-hued she-crab eggs filled the bill, adding both color and flavor. Here, from the kitchen of its birthplace, is the "official" she-crab soup recipe.

5 tablespoons butter
½ cup finely chopped celery
⅔ teaspoon ground mace
¼ teaspoon white pepper
3½ cups milk
½ cup chicken stock
5 tablespoons flour
2 cups crabmeat (see note)
1 cup heavy cream
¼ cup Worcestershire sauce
3 tablespoons sherry
Salt, if necessary, to taste
2 hard-boiled egg yolks, grated,
Paprika

1. Heat the butter in a large saucepan. Add the celery, mace, and white pepper. Cook over low heat until celery is almost transparent.

2. While celery is cooking, heat the milk and chicken stock in a small pan just enough to make the milk hot without boiling.

3. When the celery mix is done, add the flour to make a roux. Do not brown, but heat the mixture enough to bubble for several minutes.

4. Slowly add the milk and chicken stock to the roux. Add salt for taste. Add crabmeat, heavy cream, Worcestershire, and sherry. Simmer for 30 minutes or until thickened to desired consistency.

5. To serve, garnish with grated yolks, if desired. Sprinkle paprika over the top.

NOTE: "She-crabs" are known to be a real delicacy because they have much more taste than the "he-crabs." The she-crab's orange-hued eggs give the soup extra flavor and color. If she-crabs are not available in your part of the country, you may substitute white crabmeat. In this case, to create a more authentic effect, crumble a little paprika and hardboiled egg yolks in the soup to imitate she-crab eggs.

Like so many of the very best dishes, she-crab soup came to life when a few more ingredients were added for extra flavor. Now it's a staple in the South.

Think Creole!

"The word Creole in Louisiana . . . never means persons of mixed breed."
Sir Charles Lyell, 1849

~

My friend Peter Patout's patio is a colorful, tucked-away place, far from the carousing, boisterous blocks of the French Quarter the tourists know. It is a small secluded tropical paradise safe behind a wrought-iron gate and an aged masonry wall.

At the end of a narrow brick walkway dressed up with clay pots and trailing vines, orange trees bloom in March. Honeysuckle and jasmine perfume the air. And four tiers of still-green bananas gently sway in the balmy breezes. It is a mellow place.

To its serenity Peter brings humor, good cheer, contagious laughter, and the best, easiest-to-make étouffée you can imagine.

"So, Peter," I began as we finished off the first of many generous helpings, "what have you to say about Southern hospitality?"

"Think Creole! Creole!" Peter offhandedly commanded in his disarmingly easy, musical accent.

Words roll off a Creole's tongue in a lazy way. That is the charm of their dialect.

"I bet you don't even know what a Creole is," I goaded Walter.

Peter rolled his eyes at me. "I won't give him a second helping until he gets it straight," he teased, picking up Walter's plate, once again to heap it high with that delicious blend of crawfish and rice seasoned to perfection with ground red peppers.

Dear readers, the same holds true for you!

Peter's ridiculously quick, easy, and scrumptious recipe follows. But first let me tell you the true definition and origin of "Creole." It is an important word in our Southern heritage, a pure word, but over the years it has become bastardized and maligned.

A Creole is *not* necessarily a mulatto, a half-breed, or an octoroon. A Creole is a person of Spanish or French ancestry born in a colony. Most early settlers in Louisiana were Creoles—the children born in this colony of French and Spanish parents. But as they intermarried with the English, Germans, islanders, native Indians, blacks—the list goes on and on—the purity of their European line became mixed. Just a handful of Creoles married only other, pure-blooded Creoles.

Those who have studied Creole culture believe the term became jumbled when an attempt was made to distinguish between the Creoles of color (blacks who married the French and Spanish) and those blacks who did not. At any rate, these days the term Cre-

Cajun Confusion

~

If the Creoles are the aristocracy of New Orleans, who, pray tell, are the Cajuns? They are the aristocracy of a region in southwestern Louisiana known as Acadiana.

It's like this. The Creoles are descendants of French and Spanish *New Orleans* settlers. The Cajuns are descendants of French colonists who settled Acadia, Nova Scotia, in the seventeenth century. When the British claimed the land, the French who left and settled Louisiana, roughly from the Lake Charles region to Baton Rouge, likewise proudly kept their name and heritage—Cajun.

The outsider who regularly confuses and interchanges these two "Cs" may wonder what difference it makes. A lot to the Creoles and the Cajuns.

ole has become expanded to define food, land, music, language, even architecture.

But to Louisiana natives, "Creole" means a person of *pure* French or Spanish heritage. In New Orleans—La Nouvelle Orleans—the distinctive, exuberant Creole way of life has prevailed, though it is now a rich amalgamation of all cultures, all races. That's why the true Creole never misses the chance to tell you, as Peter does in his inimitable way, *"Ma chère,* my mamma is a Creole and my pappa is a Creole, and all my *cousines!"*

Now you know that, here is Peter's Mamma's recipe for pure Creole étouffée. *C'est très magnifique!*

CREOLE ÉTOUFFÉE

Serves 4 to 6

1 pound peeled crawfish tails (small shrimp may be substituted)
1 stick (8 tablespoons) butter (none other)
1 or 2 bunches green onions, sliced (tops and bottoms)
1 medium bell pepper, diced
Salt and red pepper, to taste
1 bunch fresh parsley, chopped
Long-grain rice

1. In the butter sauté the green onions with the bell pepper. Add the crawfish. Flavor with salt and red pepper to taste.

2. Allow the crawfish to simmer, covered, on the stove, stirring occasionally, for about 10 minutes. Add a full bunch of chopped parsley just before serving.

3. Prepare enough long-grain rice for 4 or 6 in a pierced, double boiler–type rice steamer. Dish up an ample portion of the crawfish over the rice.

As is often true with the simplest dishes, there are secrets. Do *not* use garlic, celery, or any seasonings included in other étouffée recipes. And take the trouble to prepare the rice correctly. The grainy texture of the rice and the pure taste of the étouffée blend perfectly.

Served with French bread, a light green salad, a dry white wine, and finished off with fresh fruit, this meal stands proud in a city known for rich creams and heavy desserts.

Incidentally, you may enjoy sharing this legend with your guests. Some say that crawfish are Yankee lobsters that moved South, where they became smaller and sweeter in the Southern waters.

And don't shrink in horror if you're asked if you want to suck the heads and pinch the tails of some "mud bugs" while you're in Louisiana. That's an invitation to feast on a crawfish boil. Dive right in!

No delight is more pleasurable than a Creole meal in the French Quarter served under the long, shadowy branches of tropical palm and banana trees. This étoufée dish offers a bit of Creole delight—wherever you are.

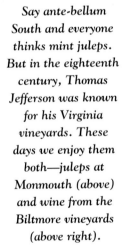

Say ante-bellum South and everyone thinks mint juleps. But in the eighteenth century, Thomas Jefferson was known for his Virginia vineyards. These days we enjoy them both—juleps at Monmouth (above) and wine from the Biltmore vineyards (above right).

Southern Spirits

EGGNOG AND MORE, TO DRINK AND TO EAT

"Before breakfast every one takes a glass of egg-nog and a slice of cake."
Emily Wharton Sinkler,
Christmas in South Carolina, 1842

Eggnog lovers hate to see the Christmas season come to an end. Who wants to give up that rich, sweet drink that the English brought with them to Virginia in the sixteenth century?

Once you had to be sick, almost dying, before you were given this delectable treat. Eggnog—full of cream and eggs and a hefty jigger of spirits—was considered medicinal. Thank goodness that's no longer the case. But don't think that eggnog can only be drunk.

Old Southern cookbooks include recipes for eggnog pie, and there is nothing better than "Comfortable French Toast," which is delicious for breakfast or for a light dinner on Christmas, after the midday feast.

But let's begin with the drink. Over the years, I have always believed that it is important to serve something wonderful in a special way that family and friends will always remember. This Christmas you, too, can experiment with unique ways of adding beauty, charm, and an individual look to your Christmas celebration.

Among my most prized family heirlooms are two nineteenth-century Victorian silver tilting pitchers—from my father's New England side of the family! Each year I bring them out with pride and use them to serve eggnog. You see, we Southerners learned "after the war" that you have to use what you have at hand.

Eggnog doesn't have to be served from the usual punch bowl—especially if you don't have one! Any favorite pitcher or beverage pot will do. This is the perfect time to bring out your family heirlooms or those items you picked up at a country auction. Try serving the eggnog in mismatched antique glasses, silver goblets, or children's baby cups—in other words, start your own new family tradition.

COMFORT EGGNOG

Serves 6

With so many commercial eggnogs available, many people have lost their grandmother's traditional recipe. Yet eggnog is ridiculously easy to make, and even if you order a catered Christmas party or dinner, this might be the one homemade treat you serve. Remember, eggnog is good without spirits, and you may want to offer your guests a choice of each type.

When reading eggnog recipes, I was amazed how many nineteenth-century recipes called for as much as a half pint and more of whiskey for every 6 eggs! Brandy, whiskey, rum—any of these spirits blend well with the basic eggnog recipe, but to me, when you add the fruity taste of that traditional Southern drink, Southern Comfort, the hint of sweetness makes the eggnog even more "Christmasy."

6 medium eggs
½ cup sugar
¾ cup Southern Comfort
1 pint heavy cream, whipped
Vanilla to taste
Grated nutmeg

1. Separate the egg whites from the yolks and place them in separate bowls.

2. Lightly beat the sugar in with the yolks. Slowly add Southern Comfort.

3. Whip the cream and add to the egg-yolk mixture. Whip the egg whites and fold into the mixture. Add vanilla to taste.

4. Pour the eggnog into a punch bowl and dust with freshly grated nutmeg.

To celebrate their 25th anniversary, the Grays of Graylyn commissioned a punch bowl embossed with scenes of their beloved home.

SOUTHERN "COMFORT-ABLE" FRENCH TOAST

~

Serves 6-8

If you are a French toast lover, this is the recipe for you. When touring for my book *Southern Christmas* in 1992, I made countless batches of Comfortable French Toast on TV shows across the country. I never had one crust of bread left to toss out! The interviewers, cameramen, and crew devoured every bite and asked for the recipe. Spenser Christian of *Good Morning America* told me he is a French toast aficionado and that this is the best he had ever tasted. I think you'll agree.

> *1 loaf French bread (baguette style)*
> *6 medium eggs, beaten*
> *1 quart Southern Comfort eggnog, either commercially bought or made from the recipe on page 153.*
> *½ teaspoon ground cinnamon*
> *½ teaspoon ground nutmeg*
> *½ cup sugar*
> *½ cup Southern Comfort (optional)*
> *¼ cup (½ stick) butter (or a nonstick spray)*

1. Cut the French bread into thick slices, approximately 2 inches each. Arrange in a long ovenproof dish and set aside.

2. Combine the beaten eggs with the eggnog. Add cinnamon, nutmeg, and, if you choose, Southern Comfort. Mix well.

3. Slowly and evenly pour the egg mixture over the French bread. Push the bread down so it will not float. Cover tightly with plastic wrap and refrigerate overnight. Turn the bread at least once so it will absorb the liquid on both sides. You can do this before going to bed if you made the mixture up earlier in the night, or first thing in the morning before you begin the cooking process.

4. Next morning preheat the oven to 350° F.

5. Melt half the butter in a heavy skillet on top of the stove (or spray the pan with a nonstick spray). Add several slices of the soaked French bread and grill until browned prettily on each side. As the slices are ready, place them in a clean ovenproof dish.

6. Meanwhile, add additional butter as needed to the skillet and complete browning all the soaked bread.

7. When the ovenproof dish is full, bake the bread for 10 to 15 minutes. The Comfortable French Toast will puff up and be ready to serve with the syrup of your choice.

EGGNOG PIE

~

Makes 1 pie

This holiday recipe appears in numerous Southern cookbooks. I think you'll enjoy the "old timey" recipe from a Coahoma, Mississippi, cookbook. Even today the combination of eggnog and lady fingers seems the epitome of a Southern dessert.

> *1½ cups whiskey*
> *12 eggs*
> *¾ cup sugar*
> *1 quart cream, whipped*
> *2 packets gelatin dissolved in 1 cup hot water*
> *1 dozen lady fingers*
> *Additional whipped cream for garnish*
> *Red and green cherries for garnish*

Colonial visitors from Europe and the North raved about the finest imported spirits found throughout the South. Southerners stored these treasured spirits in beautiful walnut cellarettes and served them in fine crystal.

1. Separate the eggs. Beat the whites stiff. Add the sugar 1 tablespoon at a time to the stiffly beaten whites.

2. Beat the yolks thoroughly. Add the whiskey a drop at a time to the yolks.

3. Fold the yolks into the beaten whites; do *not* beat. Next fold in the whipped cream. Add the dissolved gelatin.

4. Split the lady fingers into halves and use them to line a spring-form pan. Pour in the eggnog. Refrigerate for several hours. When you are ready to serve, slide the pie out of the pan and garnish with whipped cream and red and green cherries.

CLASSIC MINT JULEPS

Everyone thinks Kentucky and the Kentucky Derby have the patent on mint juleps. Far be it from me to deny or contradict that. But travel throughout the South and you'll find that mint julep stories abound.

In Mobile I learned that President James Garfield was served his first mint julep on the porch of Oakleigh in 1878. And in Richmond and Charleston I was told, "Our mint juleps are the best!"

From place to place the recipes have slight variations in the amount of sugar, the number of mint sprigs, or the choice of the essential "spirits" called for. But everywhere all true mint julep aficionados insist that once the drink is in the julep "cup," whether silver or glass, a tumbler or a tall, skinny, highball glass, the "cup" be passed on a tray, not handled, so as not to disturb the picturesque white outer frosting.

1. In a pitcher, put in 1 teaspoon sugar for each julep to be served. Dampen the sugar slightly—add just enough water to dissolve it. Into this syrup pour a hefty jigger of spirits for each julep. Add 4 to 6 mint sprigs. The exact number, and whether you leave the leaves whole or crush them, depends on how much mint taste you like.

2. While this mixture seasons, fill each individual cup with crushed or coarsely broken ice. Do not touch the outside of the container once the ice is in place. Pour the julep mixture into the glasses and stir vigorously. Let stand again for just a few seconds while the ice and julep settle.

3. Add a little more ice and stir again. By now the outside of the glasses should have a thick frosty coating. Garnish with a mint sprig and pass to your guests on a silver tray.

"Mint juleps in the morning are sent to our rooms, and then follows a delightful breakfast in the open veranda," wrote John Quitman, owner of Monmouth, in the early nineteenth century. I resisted until the cocktail hour! There are many varieties of mint julep recipes, but everyone agrees that the proper way to serve them is in a silver vessel on a tray . . . the way they still do at Monmouth.

While I chased down the history of the Ramos Fizz (above), Walter indulged in a Vick-sippi (right) like the legendary dashing riverboat travelers of long ago.

MISSISSIPPI QUEEN RAMOS COCKTAIL

One of the exquisite pleasures of a Mississippi Queen cruise is that stolen time when you do something you'd never do on a workday. For some it is sunbathing, for others a card game with new friends. For me it was taking the time to sip a late-afternoon cocktail while chatting with Matt Wilson, the bar steward. I picked up a little history, a recipe or two, and called it work . . . well, sort of.

For example, Matt told me how Antoine Amedie Peychaud, a nineteenth-century New Orleans pharmacist, concocted a special tonic he called "bitters." Like eggnog, the bitters were intended to be a medicinal remedy, but they added such a delightful zest to the cognac brandy Peychaud also served in his apothecary shop—"Only in New Orleans!" I remember thinking to myself—that soon his bitters became an essential ingredient in cocktails

served world over, and these days it's available everywhere.

Another tidbit I learned was that in New Orleans, the home of the mixed drink or cocktail, these drinks were first served in egg cups, the French word for which is coctier—leading eventually to the Americanized term "cocktail."

One of the *Mississippi Queen's* most requested drinks is a frothy Ramos Fizz. That's because people think it is too hard to prepare at home. The key is shaking it a lot—at least thirty times—so the egg whites get whipped up with the ice cubes. Here's the recipe, with a suggestion that you adjust the sugar to your taste.

Juice of ½ lemon
White of 1 egg
1 teaspoon confectioners' sugar
2 ounces dry gin
1 tablespoon heavy cream
½ teaspoon orange flower water

Shake well with cracked ice and strain into a tumbler. Fill with carbonated water and stir.

VICKSBURG VICK-SIPPI

1½ ounces Southern Comfort
¾ ounce crème de cassis
1½ ounces sweet-and-sour mix
1½ ounces 7-Up
Dash of grenadine
Ice

Combine all the ingredients in a cocktail shaker. Shake to mix all ingredients and strain into a cocktail glass. Top with a dollop of whipped cream.

Enola Prudhomme and Her Family Cajun Café

~

Some meetings along our trip were meant to be. When leaving Beaumont, Texas, we asked if there was a good restaurant nearby.

"You're going close to Carencro," our friend Matt White grinned mischievously. "Go by Enola's."

"Enola's?"

The name just didn't register at the time.

"Enola Prudhomme." Matt grinned even wider.

Need I say more?

A good three hours later we turned off of Interstate 10, followed the signs to I-49 to Opelousas, took exit 7, and soon were enjoying a serving up of Southern hospitality the likes of which you don't find every day.

From the moment we stepped in, everyone was so friendly I didn't hesitate to ask if Enola was there. She wasn't, but she was about the only family member who had skipped out a little early that night.

Our waiter was one of her sons-in-law, Chef Ike Broussard. Sheldon Prather, Enola's husband, was tending the cash register. Other waiters included Liz Vidrin, her granddaughter, and Sis Prudhomme, her sister-in-law. And last, but never least, the night's head chef was another son-in-law, Chris Oncale.

When I did catch up with Enola, she

It takes some doing to get to Opelousas, Louisiana, but Enola Prudhomme's Family Cajun Cafe, filled with generations of families past and present, lives up to its name.

shared this tale of how her melt-in-your-mouth jalapeño cheese bread came to be.

One day a former son-in-law brought Enola some good homemade cheese bread he had gotten at work. The cheese was chunky, though, and only an occasional bite was filled with that delicious cheesy flavor, Enola explained. She tried her own version and "of course I threw in some jalapeño peppers out of the garden." She laughed as if any cook would do any differently.

Sometime later Enola went to work with her famous brother, Paul Prudhomme. When she fixed the jalapeño cheese bread for him he simply said, "You need to put even more cheese and jalapeños in it."

"So I did, and it was wonderful," she exclaimed. "But"—her voice fell—"he never made any other comments about it. I wanted him to say it was the best thing he had ever tasted! Then one day he said, 'Hey, Enola, when you gonna make some more of that bread?' "

Then she half confided, half bragged that *her* bread was so good Paul put the recipe in *his* cookbook, but didn't give her the credit.

"That's okay," I laughingly assured her. "Now the truth will be known."

ENOLA'S JALAPEÑO & CHEESE BREAD

~

Makes about 18 rolls

This makes it officially Enola's recipe. If you love to make yeast rolls, you'll soon be making these for your own table and to give as gifts!

> *2 cups warm water (about 105° F.)*
> *2 ¼ ounce packets dry yeast*
> *¼ cup powdered milk*
> *¼ cup plus 2 tablespoons Crisco oil*
> *6 cups all-purpose flour*
> *2 tablespoons sugar*
> *1 teaspoon salt*
> *½ cup shredded cheddar cheese*
> *¼ cup minced jalapeño peppers*

1. In a medium bowl, combine the water, yeast, milk, and ¼ cup oil. Whisk together, then let stand for 5 minutes.

2. In a large bowl, combine the flour, sugar, and salt. Slowly add the liquid yeast mixture to the flour; mix until the flour is thoroughly incorporated. Add the cheese and jalapeños, and mix well.

3. With floured hands, place the dough onto a lightly floured surface and knead by hand for 5 minutes, or until the dough is slightly sticky to the touch.

4. Place the remaining 2 tablespoons oil in a large bowl. Add the dough, turning several times to coat with the oil. Cover the dough with a clean, dry towel; let it stand in a warm place until the dough doubles in size.

5. Remove the towel and, with your fist, punch the dough down, then place it on a lightly floured surface. Knead the dough for 5 minutes, then shape the dough into 18 rolls.

6. Place the rolls in a baking pan that has been sprayed with vegetable cooking spray. Cover again with the dry towel; allow the dough to rise until double in size again.

7. Preheat the oven to 375° F. Remove the towel and bake the dough for 45 minutes, or until golden brown on top.

CAJUN CATFISH

~

Makes 3 servings

It used to be that only Southerners ate catfish. It had long been one of our favorite traditional regional foods. These days catfish is so popular it is now one of our favorite traditional *American* foods.

I may be prejudiced, but my taste buds prefer catfish when it's prepared Louisiana style, whether Cajun or Creole. That dash of red pepper mixed with ground spices adds just the right tang to the naturally sweet catfish flavor.

Try Enola's recipe, and see if you don't agree that this is a melt-in-the-mouth treat.

> *⅛ teaspoon ground white pepper*
> *⅛ teaspoon ground oregano*
> *⅛ teaspoon ground thyme*
> *⅛ teaspoon paprika*
> *Dash ground red pepper*
> *3 3- to 5-ounce catfish fillets*
> *1 tablespoon reduced-calorie margarine*
> *1 cup thinly sliced fresh mushrooms*
> *¼ cup finely chopped green onions*
> *2 tablespoons dry white wine*
> *½ cup beef stock or water*

"The Southerners have a magnificent hospitality of the peasant and the grande: if you will take what is there you are welcome to it."
Louise Closser Hall, 1916

160

1. In a small bowl, combine first 5 ingredients and mix together well. Sprinkle the seasoning mixture on both sides of the fish and set aside.

2. In a large skillet over high heat, melt the margarine until bubbly. Add the fish and sauté for 1 minute, or until the fish is lightly browned, turning often. Add the mushrooms and green onions and cook for another time.

3. Add the wine and cook, shaking the skillet often, for 5 minutes, or until the fish flakes easily with a fork and mushrooms are tender. Add the stock and cook for 3 minutes. When the liquid is reduced by half, remove the fillets using a spatula and place them on warm serving plates.

4. Over high heat continue reducing the sauce for 3 minutes, or until it reaches a thick, rich consistency. Remove from the heat and spoon some sauce over each fillet.

Bar-b-que

THERE'S MORE THAN ONE WAY TO ROAST A PIG

"Red pepper is much used to flavor meat with the famous "barbecue" of the South and which I believe they esteem above all dishes is roasted pig dressed with red pepper & vinegar."
Sara Hicks Williams, 1853

I'll admit it: I love barbecue. And to my way of thinking (at least up until my trip to Brenham, Texas), barbecue, *true* barbecue, is chopped pork with a vinegar-based sauce. (Pickled pork, my friend Jenny Herbert calls it.) I will always have cravings for really good vinegar-based pork barbecue, and my personal favorite is that piled-high sandwich of tart, vinegary chopped pork topped with sweet,

I'll admit it. North Carolina vinegar-based bar-b-que is still my favorite, but the fellows at the North Bend Fair won over my taste buds for true Texas bar-b-que.

crunchy cold slaw and served on a spongy hamburger bun at Don Murray's Barbecue on Capital Boulevard, Raleigh, North Carolina.

I have even publicly declared, "There is no barbecue west of Raleigh, North Carolina." Even that barbecue you get in Greensboro or Danville, each just an hour and a half west of Raleigh, doesn't cut it.

When Walter discovered my passion for the distinctly Southern delicacy, he wanted to stop at every barbecue shack that popped up on our trip. It didn't matter what time it was, or whether we'd just eaten five miles down the road and ten minutes earlier.

I did nothing to discourage his on-the-road indulgence, and I'll have to say some of the barbecue we found was pretty tasty—even good. But as he licked his chops after each meal, my ending comment was always the same. "It's okay (or good, or pretty good, or not so good, as each taste test called for), but it's not *real* barbecue."

I have to retract all that now. I've been to Tex's Bar-B-Que in Brenham, Texas . And I'll say up front that you can cook some mighty good Texas-style barbecue at home. That's something you really can't do with eastern North Carolina–style barbecue. (But in all fairness, I feel that comparing my eastern North Carolina barbecue and Texas barbecue is like comparing the two states or, as the saying goes, apples to oranges. They're different.)

We ate some great barbecue ribs outdoors at the North Bend County Fair thanks to the Fort Bend Cookers. And if we hadn't dropped in at Tex's the next day, I'd probably say that the fellows at Fort Bend barbecue had won me over.

But you see, there's something special

about talking to the cook while the two of you are sitting down at a Formica table in a roadside café with organdy curtains on the windows, where the ice tea is self-serve from a twenty-gallon industrial water cooler and you scoop ice out of a gray plastic Igloo cooler. To use a million-dollar word, that "ambiance" adds flavor to barbecue.

At the fair I'd had a great teacher. Richard Harris, a prize-winning barbecuer himself, gave me my first lessons in cooking true Texas barbecue.

I learned that you cook the brisket, butt, or shoulder, or even tenderloin if your budget will allow, slowly, very slowly, basting it in a "mop" about five times during the five- to eight-hour-long baking time (according to the size and cut of the meat).

This sounds simple enough—but wait. How do you make the mop and how about the delicious sauce I had been served on the side? (Incidentally, the sauce is called "sop.")

"Well now, that's a different matter," Richard drawled. They're the *secrets* and, I was told, "Don't expect to get those recipes."

But "secrets" is what I got from Bonnie Benkowski.

She and her husband, Clarence, started Tex's Bar-B-Que twenty years ago while both worked at other full-time jobs. Ten years later they turned to cooking and catering full time. Now Bonnie's planning their next ten years.

For $4 at Tex's you get the kind of home-cooked meal your grandparents talked about and, if you're lucky, you remember from your own childhood.

Choices include: lima beans, corn, string or pole beans, greens, potatoes, pintos, squash, okra, tomatoes—when in season, country-

style steak, bar-b-que (chicken, pork, beef, sausage), fried chicken, pork chops, hamburger. . . the list goes on. You finish dinner off with a cup of pudding. (Walter ate mine.)

But on the side you're dished up smiles and laughter and a genuine love for food and people—black and white, Poles and Texans, rich and poor, town and country. The Brenham community is a mixture of all those sorts, and we all ate to our hearts contents that Sunday noontime at Tex's.

Being a Southerner myself, I knew the black gentleman seated with his wife dressed in her Sunday best at the table next to me had to be a Baptist minister. He had on a red tie. I've never known a Southern Baptist minister yet who didn't wear a red tie on Sunday.

What I didn't expect was his name. Printed on the card he gave me was "Reverend Lordy Lee Randle, Pastor, New Hope Baptist Church."

New Hope is only one of Randle's churches in this place where it isn't unusual to hear a black sprinkle a few Polish words into his conversation. They've lived side by side so long in Texas that's how they talk.

I would have liked to have visited with the Reverend Randle longer, but he had just stopped in for a little snack before moving on to another church a few miles away to lead the afternoon prayer service.

Then there was the sweat-shirt–clad matron who ran in to carry out dinner for her company due in from Houston. They said they were coming to visit, but on one condition: Supper had to come from Tex's.

Your supper can, too.

Here's the mop and the sop in as specific directions as you're going to get from a real Texas cook.

From Country's in Columbus, Georgia (opposite), to Walker's in Jackson, Mississippi (above), the food, as great as it is, is only part of the appeal. The fun of the Southern eating experience is taking a sentimental journey back in time because here, the best of yesterday is still hanging around today.

TEX'S BAR-B-QUE

Choose your cut of meat and prepare a charcoal grill to cook it on. Figure how long it will take to get thoroughly done. (For example, a Boston butt is done when the bone can be twisted right out, and a boneless brisket is ready when the meat strips away with a fork.) Cook the meat on one side—not rotisserie style—dip it in the mop about every 30 minutes, then turn.

A POTFUL OF MOP

Fill a large multigallon pot almost full of water. Pour in ample amounts of vinegar, a handful of whole allspice, several quartered onions, cut-up lemons (seeds, skin, and all), lots of salt, sticks of margarine (or butter), and the Worcestershire sauce. Cook it until it becomes so potent the fumes "make you cry." Dip the meat in the mop each time you turn it on your grill. Do not baste the meat with the mop.

Texas barbecue is served naked. Sauce is available on the side for dipping. True Texas barbecue is *never* basted with or cooked in any sauce.

SIDE SAUCE OR SOP

1½ large yellow onions, chopped
½ cup water
32-ounce bottle ketchup
1 stick (8 tablespoons) butter
½ box light brown sugar
1 lemon, juice, seeds, and all
2 cups Worcestershire sauce
Salt and pepper to taste

In a blender, blend onions with the water. Stir with the other ingredients in a large saucepan and cook for 30 to 45 minutes, or until thick. A little water can be added to get the desired consistency. Refrigerate or freeze.

Back in the eighteenth century, Southern families and neighbors gathered for outdoor pig-pickings. We aren't about to let such a time-tested tradition die! In Brenham, Texas, it is served up by Bonnie and Clarence Benkowski (right) with mop on the side. And in Chatam, Virginia, friends look forward to Eldon's fall bar-b-que all year long (above and far right).

Emeril's Chef's Bar

A couple of years ago when I called for reservations for one at Emeril's, the friendly New Orleans voice on the line asked, "Would you like to be at the Chef's Bar?"

"Oh, no," I quickly replied. "I'm coming for dinner, not drinks."

She laughed. "The Chef's Bar isn't a 'bar' bar. It's the best seat in the house, and I've only got one space left. I promise, that's where you want to be."

Now when I call Emeril's for reservations I cross my fingers and hope there will be one space left for me at the Chef's Bar. You see, there are some who would argue that a seat there is not just the best seat in the house, it's a ringside seat for one of the best shows in all of New Orleans.

There, perched high on a wooden stool, you watch fresh greens wilt over a blazing fire in a coal-black skillet. Your mouth waters as heavy cream poured into a rich brown concoction of crawfish, green onions, Worcestershire, and hot pepper sauces rises to a slow bubble in front of your very eyes. You laugh out loud as colorful peppers haphazardly sprinkled around the rim of a plate become a work of art in the hands of a master. And in no time at all you've struck up a conversation with the total strangers on your left and right. How this lively place came to

You probably won't know the people on either side of you when you sit down at Emeril's Chef's Bar. But if you finish your meal and leave without exchanging cards and conversation with your fellow diners, you've missed the chance to make a new friend.

Emeril takes special care, not only with the cooking of each dish, but with its spectacular presentation as well.

be is a simple story of true hospitality.

In his convivial Portuguese way, Chef Emeril Lagasse wanted the single diners in his restaurant to have as memorable a meal as the romantic couple at the tucked-away table and the jovial party of eight seated in the center of the room. Yet you can't just seat strangers at a table with one another—at least not in America.

"Then," Emeril told me, his flashing dark eyes lighting up as he remembered that moment, "I knew how I could do it!"

He took a wasted, dead-space corner, installed a working grill there, ran an old-fashioned counter in front of it, and put a gregarious chef behind it. Now on any given day the Chef's Bar is the noisiest, happiest spot on the floor in this always-full Warehouse District restaurant.

For a New Orleans lunch, order Emeril's and Emyl's favorite combination: Start with barbecued shrimp with biscuits, cleanse the palate with Emeril salad, feast on crawfish and corn puff pastry, and force yourself to indulge in Emeril's own favorite dessert, banana cream pie. Believe me, even if you don't like bananas, you'll find this treat delectable.

ANDRÉ'S BARBECUED SHRIMP AND HOMEMADE BISCUITS

⁓

Serves 4-6

2 pounds medium-large shrimp in their
    shells (about 42 shrimp)
2 tablespoons Emeril's Creole Seasoning
    (recipe follows)
16 turns freshly ground black pepper
2 tablespoons olive oil
¼ cup chopped onion

2 tablespoons minced garlic
3 bay leaves
3 lemons, peeled and sectioned
2 cups water
½ cup Worcestershire sauce
¼ cup dry white wine
¼ teaspoon salt
2 cups heavy cream
2 tablespoons unsalted butter
12 warm mini Buttermilk biscuits
    (recipe follows)

1. Peel the shrimp, leaving only their tails attached and reserving the shells.

2. Sprinkle the shrimp with 1 tablespoon Emeril's Creole Seasoning and 8 turns of black pepper. Use your hands to coat the shrimp with the seasonings. Refrigerate the shrimp while you make the sauce base and biscuits.

3. To prepare the sauce, heat 1 tablespoon of the olive oil in a large pot over high heat. When the oil is hot, add the onions and garlic and sauté for 1 minute. Add the reserved shrimp shells, the remaining 1 tablespoon Emeril's Creole Seasoning, the bay leaves, lemons, water, Worcestershire sauce, wine, salt, and the remaining 8 turns of black pepper. Stir well and bring to a boil. Reduce the heat and simmer for 30 minutes.

4. Remove from the heat, allow to cool for about 15 minutes, and strain into a small saucepan. There should be about 1½ cups sauce. Place the saucepan over high heat, bring the mixture to a boil, and cook until it is thick, syrupy, and dark brown, for about 15 minutes. Makes about 4 to 5 tablespoons of barbecue sauce base.

5. Heat the remaining 1 tablespoon of olive

oil in a large skillet over high heat. When the oil is hot, add the seasoned shrimp and sauté them, occasionally shaking the skillet, for 2 minutes.

6. Add the cream and all of the barbecue base. Stir and simmer for 3 to 5 minutes. Remove the shrimp to a warm platter with tongs and whisk the butter into the sauce. Remove from the heat. Makes about 2 cups.

7. To serve 6 as a first course, allow ⅓ cup sauce, about 7 shrimp, and 2 biscuits each. For 4 main-course servings, allow ½ cup sauce, about 10 shrimp, and 3 biscuits each.

EMERIL'S CREOLE SEASONING

Makes about ⅔ cup

2½ tablespoons paprika
2 tablespoons salt
2 tablespoons garlic powder
1 tablespoon black pepper
1 tablespoon onion powder
1 tablespoon cayenne pepper
1 tablespoon dried leaf oregano
1 tablespoon dried leaf thyme

Combine all ingredients thoroughly and store in an airtight jar or container. This will keep for up to 3 months.

MINI BUTTERMILK BISCUITS

Makes 12

These delicious, small biscuits are also wonderful for ham biscuits. If you make them larger than Emeril's 1-inch size, increase the baking time slightly. Follow this plain recipe for the biscuits to accompany the shrimp dish.

But for other times Emeril suggests that you flavor the recipe by adding your favorite fresh herb—thyme, tarragon, basil, cilantro, or dill—or to make cheese biscuits, add a tablespoon of grated Parmesan cheese. I suggest you may even want to turn them into biscuits, Enola Prudhomme style, by adding a little Cheddar cheese and jalapeños to the basic recipe. See page 160.

1 cup all-purpose flour, sifted
1 teaspoon baking powder
⅛ teaspoon baking soda
¼ teaspoon salt
2 tablespoons unsalted butter
¼ cup plus 1 teaspoon buttermilk

1. Preheat the oven to 375° F. Line a baking sheet with parchment or wax paper.

2. In a medium bowl, combine the dry ingredients and blend thoroughly. Cream in the butter with your fingers or a fork, until the mixture resembles coarse crumbs. Add the buttermilk a little at a time. Using your hands or a fork, work it in just until it's thoroughly incorporated and you have a smooth ball of dough. Don't overwork or overhandle the dough.

3. On a lightly floured surface, roll out the dough with a rolling pin to a circle about 7 inches in diameter and ½-inch thick. Using a small round cookie cutter or the rim of a shot glass, press out 12 1-inch rounds. If you like, you can reroll the leftover dough to make more, but their texture will be denser than the others.

4. Place the dough rounds on the baking sheet and bake them until they are golden on top and brown on the bottom, for about 15 minutes.

EMERIL'S FABULOUS BANANA CREAM PIE

~

Makes one 9-inch pie

The first time I ate at Emeril's, I asked him to select a dessert for me. I had watched as chocolate fantasies and cheesecakes were served to others, and I was not pleased when a huge slice of banana cream pie was placed before me. I like banana, but I had one serving too many of banana pudding as a child to take it seriously as an adult.

Emeril must have sensed my disappointment. "It is my favorite," he said.

What could I do? I tasted it. What could I say?

"Emeril, I never knew a banana dessert could taste like this!"

Banana Piecrust (recipe follows)
3 cups heavy cream, divided
1 small vanilla bean, split and scraped

Just a few blocks from Emeril's Warehouse District site, tropical banana trees sway in the gentle New Orleans breezes. Maybe that's why his banana cream pie tastes like none other.

1 tablespoon unsalted butter
¾ cup cornstarch
2½ cups sugar
½ teaspoon salt
5 large egg yolks
4 ripe bananas
Caramel Drizzle Sauce
*   (recipe follows)*
2 cups heavy cream whipped
*   with ½ teaspoon vanilla extract and*
*   2 teaspoons sugar*
Shaved chocolate

1. Prepare the Banana Piecrust and allow it to cool completely.

2. Heat 2 cups in a large saucepan over high heat. Stir in the paste scraped from inside the vanilla bean and the butter, and bring to a simmer.

3. Meanwhile, in a small bowl, combine the remaining 1 cup cream with the cornstarch, and stir until thoroughly blended and smooth.

4. When the mixture in the saucepan begins to boil, stream in the cream/cornstarch mixture, whisking constantly until all is thoroughly incorporated. Remove from the heat.

5. In a bowl, combine the sugar and salt, and whisk this dry mixture vigorously into the saucepan until the cream is thick and the dry ingredients are thoroughly incorporated.

6. Over low heat, whisk in the egg yolks one at a time. Remove from the heat and whisk this pastry cream until it is smooth and creamy.

7. Peel the bananas and cut them crosswise into ¼-inch slices. Spread about ⅓ of the pastry cream in the piecrust and arrange ½ of the banana slices over the cream. Spread on another ⅓ of the pastry cream and arrange the remaining banana slices over that. Cover with the remaining pastry cream and smooth out the top. Refrigerate for at least 2 hours, or until firm.

8. About 20 minutes before serving, prepare the Caramel Drizzle Sauce. (Recipe follows.) To serve the pie, cut it into wedges and drizzle on the warm Caramel Drizzle Sauce. Top with whipped cream and shaved chocolate.

BANANA PIECRUST
2 cups graham cracker crumbs
¼ cup light brown sugar, packed
1 stick (8 tablespoons) unsalted butter,
*   at room temperature*
1 very ripe banana, mashed

1. Preheat the oven to 375° F.

2. In a medium bowl, cream the ingredients together with your hands. Press the mixture into a 9-inch pie pan.

3. Bake the crust until brown, about 15 minutes. Remove the crust from the oven and allow it to cool completely before filling.

CARAMEL DRIZZLE SAUCE
1 cup sugar
¼ cup water
1 cup heavy cream

1. In a saucepan, combine the sugar and water. Bring it to a boil, stirring often. Cook, stirring occasionally, until the mixture is a deep nutty-brown color and the consistency of thin syrup, for about 10 to 15 minutes. Turn off the heat.

2. Stir in the cream, turn the heat back on to high, and boil the sauce for about 2 minutes. Remove from the heat. Use immediately.

What Becomes a Legend Most?

~

I wouldn't dream of stepping into a Baskin-Robbins or Häagen-Dazs ice cream parlor and ordering a triple scoop of their richest, creamiest confection. I have friends who tell me that they have eaten, by themselves, an entire 6-ounce bag of ranch-flavored potato chips or a large, deep-pan deluxe pizza at one sitting. Not I.

Oh, sometimes I'll sneak a Snickers or Cadbury Fruit and Nut bar when I think no one is looking. But generally speaking, I'm a moderate sort of person—until it comes to dessert in the dimly lit, Caribbean Room in New Orleans' Pontchartrain Hotel, that is.

There, after enjoying a delectable but light dinner of Snapper Eugene, I habitually smile ever so demurely at my attentive waiter

"I can't possibly eat the whole thing" everyone protests. "Bring three extra spoons," is the common request. Funny, there's never a bite of Mile High Pie left— the signature dessert of The Pontchartrain's Caribbean Room.

*Joie d' vivre—
there's no other way
to put it. Laughter,
gaiety, food, friends—
New Orleans brings
out the best in us.
Here at the Hotel
Pontchartrain, much
of the joie d' vivre is
brought by maître
d'hôtel, Douglas
Leman (above) and
chef Joel Simoneaux
(below).*

and order their signature dessert—the Jack-and-the-beanstalk-tall, extravagantly sublime, mountain of Neapolitan and peppermint ice cream encased in a pie shell, topped off with a meringue dripping with Ghiradelli chocolate sauce, and artfully garnished with plump, succulent berries.

"Mile High Pie, please," I request.

Then I whisper, "A whole slice."

That's one rich slice of pie.

I find it most appropriate that this not-to-be-equaled indulgence originated here, in the legendary dining room of the St. Charles Street hotel that has long been the scene of many rich slices of New Orleans life.

I once heard the grand old Pontchartrain Hotel referred to as "that elegant hotel without a lobby."

Its architecture may not be the best. Then again, who needs a lobby when New Orleans is your playground? You need only a quiet, luxurious room with culinary treats as close as room service or as near as the dining room downstairs.

For years that's been enough for the famous and the infamous. Anne Rice, who lives only a stone's throw away, comes often. Mick Jagger has spent Mardi Gras in the Penthouse. That's also where Tom Cruise spent part of his honeymoon. Over the years Richard Burton, Truman Capote, Zsa Zsa Gabor, Tennessee Williams ate, slept, drank, and passed time there.

And it has been enough for many not-so-famous people—folks like you and me. My parents stayed there in the 1940s. So have my children in the 1990s.

One man has watched over the generations of guests and families who continually gather in the Caribbean Room—Douglas Leman, their legendary maître d'hôtel. *Extraordinaire*, I would add.

Mr. Douglas, as he is respectfully and lovingly called, is a worldly man. He loves fine food, of course, and he knows it well. But his purest talent lies in his ability to weave spellbinding tales in a style that only a born storyteller can.

While Walter and I ate and drank, Mr. Douglas enchanted us with his memories of this place in another time.

We were treated to stories that we undoubtedly will retell over many equally memorable dinners yet to be. But we will not tell them so well. We are of another generation. We do not have Mr. Douglas' grace, nor his gift of imagery.

Poetic similes trip off his tongue. They are so perfectly phrased that only later do you realize the poignancy of his descriptions. Words like *mirth* and *blithe*, words you haven't thought of, much less heard, recently, sprinkle Mr. Douglas' conversation. This is a man of rare talents.

He, himself, is rare.

So is his love for his city, his hotel, and his Caribbean Room.

After forty-one years there, Mr. Douglas is no longer at his stand by the door to greet his guests as graciously, as comfortably, as if they were coming to his home to dinner. Rather you find him dining with guests who are thrilled to have his charming, statesman-like company.

I had been so honored twice before. The third time was the night that Walter and I dined with him. It was a velvet night of pure Southern comfort.

The hours slipped by until suddenly it was ridiculously late. We had talked incessantly while others, perhaps more prudent but less wise, had retired. Finally, when we realized that even the ever-polite staff could no longer stifle an occasional yawn, we regretfully rose to say our good-byes.

What a memorable time! We had cleaned our plates. We had drained the bottle. We had indulged in the best of human emotions and shared experiences in elegant surroundings. With Mr. Douglas we had tasted the best of life. For just a few brief hours we had captured the dream world we all long for. We had been part of a vignette of elegant Southern hospitality reminiscent of candle-lit antebellum days when food and drink, beauty and laughter, kind words and great cheer were important values to those who appreciated the good life.

New Orleans, the Pontchartrain, the Caribbean Room, Douglas Leman. It is rare to find so many legends in one place—or so many delicious choices on a menu. My favorite is the time-tested Pontchartrain favorite, Snapper Eugene. But Chef Joel Simoneaux, a petite and charming Leslie Caron look-alike, brings her Cajun background to her own specialties. For you now, here are two delicious selections. You'll have to visit the Caribbean Room to try the others—and the Mile-High Pie.

SNAPPER EUGENE WITH LEMON BUTTER

~

Serves 2

2 pieces snapper, 6 ounces each
Flour for dredging
3 tablespoons butter (preferably garlic butter)
4 jumbo shrimp, peeled and deveined
6 ounces lump crabmeat
1 tablespoon Cajun spice, available in gourmet shops
2 teaspoons Worcestershire sauce
½ cup white wine
2 teaspoons fresh lemon juice
4 ounces fresh shallots, chopped
2 teaspoons fresh parsley, chopped
½ stick butter

1. Dredge the snapper in flour. Sauté over high heat in 3 ounces of butter. Add the shrimp and crabmeat. Sauté.

2. Add the Cajun spice and cook until golden brown, about 10 to 12 minutes. Add the Worcestershire sauce, white wine, lemon juice, shallots, and parsley. Let cook and reduce for 5 minutes. Remove the seafood to a warm plate, snapper first. Top it with the shrimp and crabmeat.

3. To the juices in the pan, whisk in the fresh butter, and pour it over the fish.

An eye-catching sprinkling of finely chopped peppers and parsley around the rim of the plate remind me of Mardi Gras confetti.

CHEF JOEL'S GRILLED PORK CHOPS WITH SMOKED ORANGE AND ROSEMARY MARMALADE SAUCE

Serves 2

Say South and everyone immediately thinks bar-b-que. Many other wonderful pork dishes are elegant, delicious, and pretty. The smoked oranges make this outstanding.

2 oranges, peeled and seeded
1 quart pork (or chicken) stock
1 ounce red wine
1 tablespoon fresh rosemary leaves
½ cup orange marmalade
1 tablespoon cracked black pepper
2 9-ounce double-cut pork chops

1. To smoke the oranges, soak wood chips in water and put them in a baking pan. Place a roasting rack on top of the pan, and lay the peeled and seeded orange sections on this. Cover all with aluminum foil and place in a 350° F. oven for 30 minutes.

2. While the oranges are smoking, combine the pork stock, wine, rosemary, marmalade, and pepper. Reduce the stock by cooking it (stirring occasionally) over medium heat for approximately 40 minutes, or until the sauce coats the back of the spoon.

3. Grill the pork chops, seasoned with a pinch of salt and a double pinch of white pepper, for about 20 minutes.

4. To serve, pour the sauce over the pork chops and garnish with the smoked orange sections. A sprig of fresh rosemary also adds a lovely touch.

As the sun sets and a full hunter's moon rises, the lights come on in the Crescent City below. In this romantic setting, dinner is served on the penthouse balcony of the Pontchartrain Hotel. Every detail is perfect, including the flowers by Chopin's, a florist in business for over a century.

More Delicious Desserts

Imagine, if you can, preparing twenty or thirty different desserts only to hear a guest complain that the one delicacy he or she especially wanted to sample was gone! What would you do? Next time you would prepare even more, for in the late eighteenth century the dessert course was the showplace for a woman's culinary skills—plus her aesthetic sensibilities. Even privileged ladies with servants prided themselves on their dessert-making skills.

French and English style books of the day, not unlike our glamorous cookbooks, dictated the appropriate arrangement for the dessert table. Well turned-out dessert tables, adorned with complementary heights, shapes, textures, and colors artistically and lavishly displayed, pleased the eighteenth-century eye while enhancing the guests' hearty appetites.

With an ample supply of pears, apples, peaches, grapes, and walnuts and pecans from the plantation orchards, sugar and spices from the islands, and of course flour, eggs, milk, and butter readily available, the Southern woman had everything she needed to create quite an array of cakes, puddings, tarts, jellies, trifles, creams, and syllabubs.

The tradition lives on. Ask a Southerner, "Will you have cake or pie or ice cream?" and the reply, at least at holidays, will often be "Yes." After all, a little self-indulgence is good for the spirit. Why, a life without chocolate and cream and pecan pie smacks of days of self-depriving Puritanism to me!

EATING MY WAY THROUGH THE SOUTH

DOUBLE-LAYERED PEACH-PECAN PIE

Makes four 9-inch pies

One day my editor called. "*Family Circle* wants your pecan pie recipe," she said.

"Tell them to get a bottle of Karo syrup and copy it off of there," I replied.

"You don't understand." Sharon tried to explain. "They want your *Southern* recipe."

"Look, Sharon, that is my recipe, and every other honest Southern cook's. It's best and it's foolproof."

Well, despite my boasting about plain, undoctored-up pecan pie, I do have to admit that the Double-Layered Peach-Pecan Pie I had at the St. Francisville Inn, in St. Francisville, Louisiana, was so good that I literally licked my fork when I could not find one more morsel to consume on my plate.

6–7 *large, ripe peaches, chopped*
¾ *cup sugar*
½ *teaspoon ground cinnamon*
¼ *teaspoon ground cloves*
4 *medium eggs, beaten*
¾ *cup brown sugar, packed*
¾ *cup dark Karo syrup*
3 *teaspoons butter, softened*
2 *teaspoons vanilla extract*
½ *teaspoon salt*
1 *tablespoon imitation peach syrup or*
    peach Schnapps (optional)
8 9-inch-deep *pie crusts*
1½ *cups pecans, chopped*
2½ *cups pecan halves*

1. Preheat the oven to 350° F.

2. In a large saucepan, cook the peaches and sugar (no water!) over medium heat until they

are soft and thick. This will take some time. They should not be runny. If necessary, add a little cornstarch to thicken. Stir in the cinnamon and cloves. Set the fruit mixture aside to cool.

3. In a medium bowl, combine the eggs, brown sugar, Karo syrup, butter, vanilla, salt, and peach syrup. Set aside.

4. Cover the bottom of four of the pie shells with the chopped pecans. Over them spoon enough of the egg/sugar mixture to coat the pecans. (Use about 6 ounces for all four pies.) Place a second pie crust over the first. Press the sides and top of the pie crusts together, slightly building up the sides. Remove any excess dough and indent with knife tip. Cut several slits into middle of the top pie dough.

5. Add the pecan halves and peaches to the remaining egg/sugar mixture and mix well. Spoon equal portions onto the top of each pie.

6. Bake for approximately 45 minutes, or until the pies are golden brown and when a knife (or broom straw) comes out clean.

Like the famed provincial foods of Europe, delectable gourmet dishes can be found on out-of-the-way streets throughout the South. The double-layered peach-pecan pie at the St. Francisville Inn in northwestern Louisiana was one of my favorite dishes on the entire trip.

A true Florida Key Lime Pie is a refreshingly cool, citrusy tart treat any time of year.

BREAKERS KEY LIME PIE

Makes one 8-inch pie

Don't be fooled by those imitation, sweet minty-green pies you're served in New York and Boston. True Florida Key Lime Pies are lemony yellow and citrusy tart. They're also so easy to make that you'll pull this recipe out time after time. It is a standard at the elegant Breakers. Why not at your house?

> 1 8-inch pie shell
> 3 cups sweetened condensed milk
> 3 medium egg yolks
> ⅔ cup fresh lime juice

1. Preheat the oven to 350° F.

2. Prebake the crust until it is light in color. Mix the condensed milk and egg yolks until they are just combined. Add the juice and mix well. The mixture will tighten as it sits.

3. Pour the mixture immediately into the cooked pie shell. Bake for approximately 10 to 15 minutes. The mix will still be soft. Refrigerate for 4 hours to set before serving.

CHOCOLATE BUTTERMILK LAYER CAKE

Makes one 2-layer cake

1 stick (8 tablespoons) butter
1¼ cups sugar
2 medium eggs
2 1-ounce squares baking chocolate, melted
1¾ cups all-purpose flour
1 teaspoon baking soda
1 teaspoon salt
1 cup buttermilk

1. Preheat the oven to 350° F.

2. Cream the butter and the sugar. Add 1 egg at a time and beat after each. Add the melted chocolate.

3. Sift the flour 3 times with baking soda and salt. To the butter/sugar mixture, add the flour alternating with the buttermilk, and ending with flour.

4. Pour the batter into 2 8-inch round wax paper–lined or Teflon layer pans. Bake for 30 minutes. Cool and ice with Fudge Icing.

FUDGE ICING

2 cups sugar
⅓ cup unsweetened cocoa
¼ teaspoon salt
½ cup milk
½ cup (1 stick) margarine
1 teaspoon vanilla extract

1. In a medium saucepan over medium heat, bring the first 5 ingredients to a rolling boil. Boil the mixture for 2 minutes.

2. Remove from the stove. When cool, add the vanilla and beat until shiny.

LAURA'S VISITING PIE

Serves 8 to 10

4 eggs
1 cup sugar
1 cup light corn syrup
½ cup butter, melted
1 cup English walnuts, chopped
½ cup semisweet chocolate chips
2 teaspoons bourbon or 1 teaspoon vanilla
* extract*
1 uncooked 9-inch pie shell

1. Preheat the oven to 450° F.

2. In a large mixing bowl, beat the eggs with a fork. Add the sugar. Blend in the corn syrup, melted butter, walnuts, chocolate chips and bourbon (or vanilla).

3. Pour the mixture into the pie shell. Bake for 10 minutes, then reduce the heat to 350°F. and bake an additional 40 minutes, or until the filling is set. Cool completely. (If desired and the pie isn't "traveling," top with fresh whipped cream.)

AMBROSIA

For those who have eaten their fill of oysters, sweet potatoes, and ham, ambrosia adds a sweet taste to the palette until the diner has room for a real dessert. There are no proportions, so grate the coconut first and then add the orange sections to your own liking.

Fresh coconut
Oranges
Confectioners' sugar

1. Grate the meat of a fresh coconut. (It must be grated, not ground.) Set aside.

2. Peel the best, juiciest oranges available and carefully separate them into sections. Cut each section into two or three pieces.

3. Drain the juice. To the juice add a little confectioners' sugar (to taste).

4. Put the coconut, orange sections, and liquid in a bowl and toss lightly. The ambrosia should be moist but never runny. Chill in the refrigerator. It is prettiest when served in a crystal bowl—preferably your granny's.

The Southern sweet tooth has long been legendary. Even wealthy Southern ladies considered dessert-making an art and offered their guests many treats.

In Plant City, Florida, big, plump strawberries are ready for dipping in mounds of whipped cream in late February. What better excuse to have a county fair?

Strawberries

"Sup'd on Crabs & an elegant dish of Straw-berries & cream—How natural, how agree-able, how majestic this place seems!"
Philip Vickers Fithian, writing on May 28, 1774, from Nomini Hall, Virginia

Gathering plump, fragrant red strawber-ries bunched beneath ruffly green leaves in a Southern country meadow is a delight for anyone at any age. A pint or a quart of the sugar-sweet strawberries is reward enough in itself—but when you add a bouquet of white daisies that dot the grassy knoll, the low hum of honeybees darting by on the gentle wind, and cheerful springtime songs sung by wood-land sparrows and wrens—then you have all the best of a Southern spring day gathered in your basket of memories.

I have only a few such cherished memo-ries from childhood days in Moore County, North Carolina, and later, teenage treks to a strawberry patch near Madison, North Caro-lina. So when my father said, "Let's go for a drive and get some strawberries," last summer when I was visiting Danville, like a child, I was the first one in the car.

The ultimate strawberries aren't only those served with a Devonshire cream at an elegant English high tea. Even John Smith was impressed with the strawberries he found growing wild in Virginia. On April 22, 1607, he reported that friendly Indians met his small band of explorers by "kindely intreating us, daunsing and feasting us with strawberries."

Soon Northerners echoed Smith's high praise for this most abundant and delicious Southern springtime delicacy. To Henry Bar-

nard, a New Englander, they were the perfect ending to his dinner in Beaufort, South Caro-lina, on April 30, 1833. "I spent the evening delightfully . . . and was served with the most delicious luxury I ever met with, and that was a dish holding 4 or 5 quarts of large, ripe straw-berries, a dish of sweet cream and a bowl of fine white sugar. I never tasted anything so very fine." He then noted, "They have had strawberries for 3 weeks. . . . This is the first time in my life, that I have tasted of strawber-ries and green peas in April."

If you're in Plant City, Florida, at the end of February, you can have freshly picked strawberries two full months earlier. The an-nual Florida Strawberry Festival is a grand excuse not just for eating strawberries and bar-becue, corn dogs, pit-smoked chicken, ribs— all the country carnival fare —while visiting with friendly folks and enjoying toe-tapping country music.

We planned one leg of our Southern trek to coincide with the final day's judging of the best strawberry recipes. What a wonderful, relaxing time I had with old friends and new—Chef Tel, Steve Ott, Caroline Stuart, and my good friend Laura York from Tampa's WFLA, among others.

True to the best that Southern hospital-ity has to offer, I left with a flat of ripe, tasty strawberries, a tummy filled with hefty serv-ings of all the finalists' recipes, (a kiss from Billy Dean) and Laura's own "Visiting Pie" (see page 175) so called because, in the days before air-conditioning, it could travel long distances in the car without spoiling. Hers was the perfect gift for this pair of always hungry Southern gypsies. Eat it as Walter and I did, with bites of fresh strawberries to add a tang to its rich, velvety flavor.

SIMPLY IRRESISTIBLE STRAWBERRY SHORTBREAD

Makes 12 generous servings

This recipe comes from Lisa Sizemore of Tampa, Florida. The strawberry sauce and maple nuts may be made one day in advance.

STRAWBERRY SAUCE

2 quarts fresh Florida strawberries, divided: 1st quart: stemmed, cleaned, and mashed; 2nd quart: stemmed, cleaned, and sliced
1 cup sugar
2 tablespoons strawberry preserves
1 tablespoon cornstarch
1 tablespoon water

1. Combine 1st quart of mashed berries with sugar in a medium saucepan. Bring to a boil over medium-high heat, then reduce the heat to medium-low and simmer for 10 minutes, stirring frequently. Skim the foam.

2. Remove the pan from the heat. Stir in the preserves. In a small cup, mix cornstarch and water; add this to the berry sauce.

3. Return the pan to the stove and cook until the mixture thickens, stirring constantly. Remove from heat and reserve.

SHORTBREAD

²/₃ cup confectioners' sugar
2 cups unbleached all-purpose flour
½ pound (2 sticks) unsalted butter, chilled
1 tablespoon fresh lemon zest

1. Preheat the oven to 350° F.

2. Sift the confectioners' sugar and flour together into a food processor bowl fitted with a steel blade.

3. Cut each stick of butter into 8 pats. Drop the pats onto the dry ingredients. Pulse the food processor on and off until fine crumbs form (about 30 pulses). (Or use a pastry blender or 2 knives to cut the butter into the flour.) Stir in the lemon zest.

4. Pat the crumbs into the bottom of a lightly greased 9- x 13-inch pan. (Note: The mixture will be very dry.) Bake on the middle rack of the oven for 30 minutes.

5. Then open the oven and spread 1 cup of Strawberry Sauce onto the shortbread. Close the oven and continue to bake for 15 minutes. Remove the shortbread from oven and cool.

FILLING

6-ounce package cream cheese, softened
¼ cup confectioners' sugar
1 tablespoon half-and-half
1 teaspoon fresh lemon juice

With an electric mixer set to high, beat all the ingredients together until well blended and creamy. Then set aside.

MAPLE NUTS

1 cup walnuts toasted in 350° F. oven for 7 minutes, then coarsely chopped
⅓ cup maple or maple-flavored syrup

Combine the walnuts and syrup.

TO ASSEMBLE

1. Mix the remaining quart of sliced strawberries with the remaining cup of Strawberry Sauce; spoon onto the cooled shortbread.

2. Dollop, spread, or pipe (Lisa likes a lattice design) the cream cheese topping onto the strawberry layer. Sprinkle with the maple walnuts. Chill for 30 minutes to 1 hour before serving. It keeps well for a couple of days.

After the necessary picture-posing session, Laura York couldn't wait another minute to gobble down a taste of Lisa Sizemore's prize-winning recipe. Laura's own "Visiting Pie" (page 175) isn't too bad either!

New Year's Day

*"Mrs. Perkins, watching the beating of eggs
and stirring of the golden filling, the deft
mixing of pastry, grew cheerful and entertaining. She forgot to complain of her neighbors,
and was surprised into the telling of some of
her girlish experiences that actually brought an
amused twinkle to her sharp old eyes. . . . It
gave her a warm inward glow of satisfaction."*

Mary Johnston,
Little Colonel's Christmas Vacation

If you're going to cook only one genuine
Southern meal this year, make sure it's the traditional New Year's Day dinner. It's easy, delicious, gives you the perfect excuse to avoid
the TV ball games, and even promises to bring
you good luck through the rest of the year!

Believe me, cooking New Year's Day's

NEW YEAR'S DAY
MENU

Black-eyed Peas for Good Luck

Greens for a Prosperous Year
(You'll get a dollar for every green you eat. Then again,
some people say you'll get a dollar for every black-eyed pea.
So to be safe, eat lots of both.)

Okra and Tomatoes   Grated Sweet Potato Pudding (see page 180)

Cornbread Muffins (see page 181), with a silver dollar baked in

Cheese grits (see page 180)

Virginia Ham   Country Sausage

Pecan Pie and leftover Christmas goodies
(see Desserts, pages 172–175)

dinner can give you that "warm inward glow
of satisfaction" if you'll dive right in and indulge yourself in the process. How? While
you're working in the kitchen, pop *The Big
Easy* or *Coal Miner's Daughter*, *Fried Green
Tomatoes*, or even *Cat on a Hot Tin Roof*—
whatever your favorite Southern movie is—
into the VCR. Or put a zydeco or country and
western tape or CD on. Then relax and enjoy the cooking, the smells, the tastes, and the
lore of this, the South's most traditional meal.
We call it "feel-good food."

I'm giving you the easiest way to make a
good-tasting, thoroughly Southern New
Year's dinner. Serve it up with lots of relishes,
pickled okra, watermelon pickle, pickled
peaches, fig preserves, and a cruet of vinegar
on the side. These are wonderful accompani-
ments and found on every Southern "slab," or
huntboard or table.

BLACK-EYED PEAS

Serve 6-8

The quickest and easiest way to fix a bowl of
peas is to doctor up canned ones.

2 16-ounce cans black-eyed peas
Piece of side meat or fatty ham
1 red pepper pod (or ⅛ teaspoon cayenne
pepper)

1. Drain the liquid from 2 cans of peas into a
medium saucepan. (Put the peas into a medium mixing bowl and refrigerate until you're
ready to add them to the liquid.) Add a piece
of side meat or some fatty strips cut from the
Virginia ham you're serving, along with a red
pepper pod (or ⅛ teaspoon cayenne pepper).
Bring this to a boil and then simmer for about
10 minutes.

2. Throw in the peas, cover, and cook over low heat for 20 to 30 minutes before serving.

To fix peas from scratch, buy dried peas and follow the cooking instructions on the package. Be sure you include the flavorful fat meat and hot peppers in the seasoning.

GREENS

Serves a crowd

Collards, turnip greens, curly kale—all have distinctly different flavors. I like them mixed together. The cooking directions are the same, whether you are preparing one type or mixing them. The secret is to drain off water when cooking.

> *3 pounds greens*
> *Slab of side meat, 1 ham hock,*
> *   or 3 pieces thick-sliced bacon*
> *Salt to taste*
> *1 red pepper pod*
> *3 turnips (optional)*

1. Begin by washing and trimming several large bunches of greens. (I recommend about 3 pounds total to serve eight people.) It looks like a lot, but they cook down. It usually takes two, sometimes three, washings in salt water to remove the gritty sand and dirt from freshly picked greens—even those sold in the grocery store. That's the time-consuming part. While washing, strip the stringy stems from the leafy part and discard them.

2. During this washing time, bring 4 or 5 cups salted water to a rapid boil in a large pot on the stovetop. To salt the water, add the slab of side meat (often called a steak of fat and streak of lean), a ham hock, or several pieces of thick-sliced bacon, plus a small amount of

extra salt. (You can use a smaller amount of meat and a large helping of beef bouillon, but that's not the Southern way.) Toss in a pod of red pepper.

3. Add the washed greens a few at a time. Stir them around to "wilt" the just-added leaves. They will cook down rapidly, making room for more. Cover and cook on medium-low heat until tender, or for at least an hour, often longer. Taste the greens while they are cooking, drain extra water and add more salt if desired. For a heavy turnip flavor, add several tender peeled and quartered turnips during the last 15 or 20 minutes.

4. To serve, drain the liquid (and save to store any leftover greens in). Put the greens in a large bowl (with the turnips), and watch any Yankees present politely take just a pinch until they find out how delicious they are. Then they'll take seconds.

The traditional New Year's Day meal—Southern style—takes a little time to put together, but it's a fool-proof, no-trouble, good-luck, feel-good meal that gets the New Year off to a hospitable start to last for the next 364 days.

GRATED SWEET POTATO PUDDING

I included this recipe in *Southern Christmas*. I received at least ten letters from close friends who told me they had lost their mother's recipe for this simple and pure sweet potato dish and were forever grateful that they can now prepare it once again. There is no coconut, no orange juice, no marshmallow in this recipe. And it's a taste-and-season-as-you-go dish. (Note that all ingredients are given in approximate quantities.)

¼ teaspoon each ground cloves, allspice, ginger, nutmeg for each spice boil, plus extra to taste
½ teaspoon ground cinnamon for each spice boil, plus extra to taste
Cinnamon sticks (optional)
1½ cups water for each spice boil
3–4 bright orange sweet potatoes
1 stick (8 tablespoons) butter
½ cup Karo syrup, light
½ cup brown sugar, packed
Pinch salt

1. In a small saucepan, mix the ¼ teaspoon of the spices plus the ½ teaspoon cinnamon and the cinnamon sticks (optional) in the water. Bring this to a boil over medium-high heat, then turn the heat down to a simmer. This "spice boil" creates a wonderful scent while you are grating the potatoes and will be used later.

2. Preheat the oven to 350° F.

3. Peel the sweet potatoes; then, in a food processor, grate them. Place the grated potatoes in a large mixing bowl.

4. To the spice boil add butter, Karo syrup, brown sugar, and salt. Stir while the butter melts. Remove the cinnamon sticks.

5. Pour the spice boil/sugar mixture over the sweet potatoes and blend well. Turn into a buttered casserole dish and bake for about 30 minutes.

6. Start another round of the spice boil to keep the kitchen fragrant and to add to the pudding as needed.

7. Remove the pudding from the oven, stir well, lick the spoon, and decide if it needs more spices. If more liquid is needed, add some of the spice boil. Otherwise, just add additional ground cloves, allspice, ginger, nutmeg, and cinnamon to taste. You can also add more sugar and Karo syrup for sweeter potatoes.

8. Repeat this stirring and licking-the-spoon process every so often until you are happy with the flavor. Cook for about 1½ hours. I like a nice, browned top, but you may wish to cover the casserole dish to speed up the cooking time.

(At this point I start another round of the spice boil to keep the kitchen fragrant and to add to the pudding as needed. After the pudding has cooked for about 30 minutes, take it out of the oven, stir well, lick the spoon and decide if it needs more spices. If more liquid is needed pour in some of the spice boil. Otherwise, just shake in more ground nutmeg, ginger, allspice, and cinnamon to your liking.)

CHEESE GRITS

There aren't many dishes tastier than this one. Even the most adamant grits-hater will ask for the recipe. This much serves 6 to 8

How many more dashes of hot sauce? You can add more at the table!

moderate eaters, and the recipe can be doubled. If you prefer more cheese and less garlic flavor, you may want to use sharp Cheddar cheese and garlic powder or paste (to taste).

1 cup grits (quick cooking, not instant)

3 cups water

1½ cups milk

¼ cup (½ stick) butter

¼ teaspoon salt

6 ounces garlic cheese or sharp Cheddar,
  cut up

2 eggs, beaten

Dash Worcestershire sauce

Dash Tabasco

Cayenne pepper to taste

1. Preheat the oven to 350° F.

2. In a heavy saucepan, boil the grits in the water, milk, salt, and butter. Stir often until the mixture is stiff.

3. Then stir in the cheese pieces. Remove from the heat and allow to cool slightly.

4. Stir in the well-beaten eggs, Worcestershire, Tabasco, and pepper to taste. Spoon into a well-buttered casserole. Bake until bubbly, or about 30 minutes.

CORNBREAD MUFFINS

Makes 1 dozen

The secret is *no sugar.* When you add sugar to cornmeal, you end up with Yankee Johnny Cake, not Southern cornbread. Use yellow meal, not white. Remember the baby in the King Cake (p. 42) Bake in a silver dollar or two to begin the New Year with the guarantee of good luck for one or all.

1 cup yellow cornmeal

2 teaspoons baking powder

¾ teaspoon salt

1 medium egg, beaten

¾ cup buttermilk

½ cup cold water

1. Preheat the oven to 450° F.

2. Sift the dry ingredients together.

3. Beat the egg and buttermilk together and add the cold water. Stir the liquid into the dry ingredients. Mix thoroughly.

4. Put a heavy 12-muffin pan into the oven for just a few minutes to heat it up.

5. Remove the pan and grease it. Pour in the cornbread mixture, filling each cup about ¾ full. Bake for about 20 minutes, or until done. Before serving, top each hot muffin with a pat of butter.

It's the secret ingredients (like silver dollars baked into the corn bread) and the condiments—jars of pickles and chow-chow, that add fun and flavor to everyday dishes.

Next day we proceeded to the plantation of one of our obliging Charleston friends, who,
in the style of hospitality universal in the South, had begged us to make it a resting place.
Captain Basil Hall of Edinburgh, Scotland, March 6, 1828

The Tradition Continues

After spending over half a year traveling the highways and byways of the southern United States, Walter and I were beginning to wind down our grand adventure. ⟶ We had begun our travels on a rainy, winter day. It was now well into summer. Our next-to-last trip would be a return trip to rediscover Rosedown in St. Francisville, Louisiana, where we would shoot the cover of the book. ⟶ Why did we not go to yet another place—somewhere we had not been—or why hadn't we taken the shot when we were in St. Francisville the first time? ⟶ The story begins on our first visit there.

It was a cloudy, early March day when the *Mississippi Queen* docked at St. Francisville, just long enough for her passengers to take in a couple of sights. (No, not every Southern day is a sunny day, though most are.) Walter and I were among those who boarded the tour bus and traveled down Main Street of the sleepy little town known as "two miles long and two blocks deep."

That's a pretty accurate description of this Mississippi River village where charming Victorian houses with spacious front porches and frilly fences line each side of its two quaint streets. The backyards of the houses on the river side go down to the water. On the other side they lead into the woods.

Our first stop was beautiful Grace Episcopal Church. Walter, his camera already poised, instantly disappeared into the thick grove of century-old trees made all the more beautiful by the ancient, ivy-covered grave markers and monuments.

I followed the group inside. There, in the stillness of the sanctuary, our guide wove mesmerizing stories of the church, the village, and its people in her lilting Louisiana accent. We sighed, we laughed (quietly), we wiped away an occasional tear as we, too, relived St. Francisville's brightest and darkest moments.

The stories were so captivating that I slipped out the side door and began searching for Walter. I didn't want him to miss them.

Not surprisingly, I found him crouching on the ground to catch the juxtaposition of bright sun and dark shadow meeting at the perfect angle against a weathered stone wall.

"You've *got* to come inside!" I gushed. "You're missing wonderful stories. The Bohemian glass windows were the gifts of a Yan-

My memories of my travels through the South are rich and varied. There was the comfort of the inns (above) and the mementos of our Southern heritage (below)...

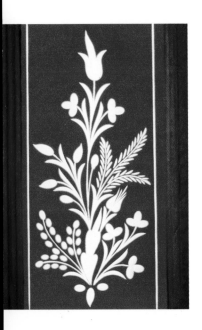

kee who shelled the church from the river during the Civil War. I told you my best stories about Southern hospitality come from Yankees!"

"Just one more shot out here first," he pleaded.

I had grown used to that response by now, and, as always, once I saw *his* discoveries, I had a hard time pulling us both away. That was typical of so many of our days. Stories and pictures—an untold wealth of riches—are everywhere in the South.

By the time we got inside, our group had disbanded and was boarding the bus. Walter hurriedly began taking pictures while I ran out wildly waving and calling, "We're coming!"

Thank goodness our fellow *Mississippi Queen* travelers were used to us by now and good-naturedly took our ways in stride.

Our next stop was Rosedown.

Looking back on that March day, Walter and I now laugh about how this was one of the few times when everything seemingly was working against us.

The gray, damp weather certainly was not cooperating. Without a car to transport the camera equipment, Walter had to make do with what the two of us could carry. Not having our own car also meant we had to keep to the tour schedule. We'd have only about an hour at Rosedown. I had made an appointment with the publicity director, Will Mangham, but when we arrived we learned he had been delayed. By now our attitudes were not the best.

We had seen so many other stunning homes from Delaware to Texas that we were debating whether to bother leaving the gift shop, especially since it was now drizzling.

We were still milling around when Will

drove up, hopped out of his car, ran over to us, and simultaneously thrust his hand out to Walter and kissed me on the cheek.

"Isn't Rosedown the most beautiful place you've ever seen? Well, come on. You've got to see all of it. Now what can I do for you? How long are you here for? Let's find the bus driver first. I'll take you back to the *Queen*," Will's words exploded in one long breath.

It's strange how one person can light up a room or change your whole way of looking at things with his vitality and enthusiasm. That's what Will Mangham had just done.

Suddenly we were swept up by the enchantment of this place. With his excitement, Will had lifted the veil of our complacency and opened our eyes to the beauty of Rosedown, the quintessential plantation home of the deep South.

What is Rosedown's charm? You might as well ask a suitor what makes his beloved his chosen one. How do you describe true love and intimate rapture? You don't. You can't.

Let it suffice to say Rosedown's quiet, still beauty is breathtaking. Her grandeur is awe-inspiring. Great canopies of cascading trees adorn her sweeping grounds. Along her winding pathways evocative statues lure you closer. At every turn mounds of blue and pink hydrangeas intermingled with webs of thick, hunter-green boxwood delight your eye.

Yet despite the grandness of her setting, Rosedown is inviting and warm, with sparkling fanlights and tall, sunny windows. This is a place, you are sure, where elegant people lived gracious lives, where lively conversation was a way of life, and where noble deeds saw its inhabitants through good times and bad.

In one short hour Will introduced us to the dedicated people who keep Rosedown the

vital place it remains today—docents, staff, volunteers. These, too, were elegant people, kind people. They were full of good cheer and lively conversation. They couldn't do enough for us. We were enamored.

Such is the Rosedown we saw and fell in love with—and vowed to return to.

As we waved good-bye to Will and dashed up the gangplank of the paddleboat just as the steam from the calliope whitened the gray sky, we, like MacArthur, promised to return.

"And you'll come to dinner at my house! Eda and I are just at-home people," I heard Will shout before the music drowned him out.

Three and a half months later we were sitting around Will and Eda's comfortable dining-room table.

This time Ken Sansone from my publishing house had joined us. Eda and Ken are of Italian stock. Will, Walter, and I are Anglo-Saxon Southerners. (Well, Walter and I *are* part Yankee.) Together we sipped wine, exchanged stories, talked about Rosedown, toasted New Orleans, laughed, and we ate Will's étouffée.

"Mmmmmm." Walter smacked his lips.

"You *are* going to give me the recipe," I said, catching Ken's nodding head out of the corner of my eye.

"There's nothing special about it," Will began modestly. Then, in his gregarious way, he broke into telling me the secret to its goodness.

"You take a stick of butter . . ."

I laughed out loud. How many times had I heard that phrase over the past few months? Peter Patout had said the same thing about his étouffée. The cook at Walnut Hill insisted that a stick of butter was the secret to her pot

...the flowers, the homes, the food, and the little things that make life pleasant.

While we were at Rosedown to shoot the book jacket, Patsy Dreher was always doing special things to make our lives more pleasant (below).

Now, That's Southern Hospitality

"Not until you come here can you imagine how entirely different is their mode of living from the North. They live more heartily."
Sara Hicks Williams, 1853

⁓

When it comes down to it, no one can tell you about Southern hospitality better than a Northerner.

What's the saying? If you want to really learn about a place, go there.

That's what Dave and Karen Smith from Oconomowoc, Wisconsin, did. They came South. Then they wanted *us* to know just how grand our Southern hospitality really is, so they wrote a letter to the newspaper in my hometown, Danville, Virginia—a 50,000-plus person textile-and-tobacco town with a heart as big as its 43.678 square miles, and a special love for stockcar racing and baseball.

When the Atlanta Braves announced they were sending a farm team to Danville, you would have thought that the Braves themselves were moving up from Georgia. Danville built a park and a stadium, and the whole town came out to that field of dreams. But it didn't stop there. Let the Smiths tell you about it.

The new park and baseball facility overlooking your lovely city are truly first class and a real tribute to the people of Danville. As parents of a young Braves player, we very much appreciated the opportunity our son, Sean Smith, had to play in your city. We appreciated, particularly, the warmth and hospitality with which you adopted our young players and made them feel welcome, even though many were thousands of miles from their families and homes.

Some of you opened your homes to them; others helped find them apartments. Thousands of you filled the stadium every home game. We were fortunate to be in Danville for the opening ceremonies and were overwhelmed with the fan enthusiasm and the park's beauty.

Being from the North, the term Southern hospitality is something that we have only heard about. We know now, firsthand, that it's much more; it's a real warm, honest way of treating people and making them feel at home. It was a great season, a great group of young players, a great Braves organization and just the greatest facility and fans you could ever ask for. Thanks, Braves, and thanks everyone in Danville!

Dave and Karen Smith
Oconomowoc, Wisconsin

pie. Chef Joel said a stick of butter will make even a bad recipe good. So had Bonnie Benkowski in Brenham, Texas.

A stick of butter may be a Southern cook's best friend. But to me, a guest in the Manghams' home, Will's quip became one of those moments frozen in time I'll always remember.

You see, the instant Will said "You take a stick of butter," joyful memories of this unforgettable journey through the South flooded before my mind's eye. And in that twinkling of a moment, the richness of a stick of butter and all it stands for—taking what you have and turning it into something wonderful, sharing your best with friends old and new—caught the heart, the roux, the elixir of Southern hospitality.

My search for the essence of those time-tested words accidentally began on a Virginia streetcorner when a stranger turned a salad into a sandwich for my convenience.

From that point on I had discovered the gift of Southern hospitality everywhere—in the yellowed pages of long-forgotten books, on the front porch swing in Ocala, Florida, in the Dallas–Fort Worth airport, on board the great *Mississippi Queen*, behind an extravagant mask at Mardi Gras in Mobile, at the simple sunrise Easter service in Old Salem, along country roads that stretch north and east of Brenham, Texas.

Yes, Southern hospitality lives beyond the city limits of my Southern hometown. It lives in the hearts of all Southerners, wherever they may be.

It is our heritage, our tradition. It is our mind-set, our way of life.

The secret? You take a stick of butter . . .

⁓

*But most of all,
I'll always
remember the
people, the
families, the
conversations,
the celebrations.
That's what
Southern
hospitality is
all about.*

Directory

Stanton Hall
High St.
Natchez, MS 39121
601-442-6282

Susina
Rte. 3, Box 1010
Thomasville, GA 31792
912-377-9644

Union Station Hotel
1001 Broadway
Nashville, TN 37203
615-726-1001

HISTORIC HOMES AND GARDENS

Afton Villa Gardens
U.S. 61
St. Francisville, LA 70775
504-635-6773

Anne Spencer House
1313 Pierce St.
Lynchburg, VA 24501
804-845-1313

Beauregard-Keyes House
1113 Chartres St.
New Orleans, LA 70116
1-504-523-7257

Berkeley Plantation
Rte. 2, Box 390
Charles City, VA 23030
804-829-6018

Beauvoir
2244 Beach Blvd.
Biloxi, MS 39531
601-388-1313

Bellingrath Gardens and
   Home
12401 Bellingrath Garden
   Rd.
Theodore, AL 36582
205-973-2217

Biltmore Estate
1 North Pack Square
Asheville, NC 28801
800-543-2961

Bluff Hall
North Commissioners Ave.
Demopolis, AL 36732

Catalpa
U.S. 61
St. Francisville, LA
504-635-3372

Colonial Williamsburg
P.O. Box Drawer GB
Williamsburg, VA 23187
800-368-6511

Danville Museum of
   Fine Arts & History
   (Last Capital of the
   Confederacy)
975 Main St.
Danville, VA 24541
804-793-5644

FDR's Little White
   House
Rte. 1, Box 10
Warm Springs, GA 31830
404-655-3511

Grace Episcopal Church
Ferdinand St.
St. Francisville, LA 70775
504-635-4065

Green-Melrim House
Bull St. on Madison
   Square
Savannah, GA 31401
912-232-1251

Henry B. Plant Museum
(Tampa Bay Hotel)
401 W. Kennedy Blvd.
Tampa, FL 33606
813-254-1891

Henry Morrison Flagler
   Museum
Cocoanut Row
Palm Beach, FL 33480
407-655-2833

Houmas House
40136 Hwy.
942 Burnside
Darrow, LA 70725
504-473-7841

John C. Calhoun House
   Museum
Fort Hill
Clemson University
Clemson, SC 29634
803-656-2475

Juliette Gordon Low Girl
   Scout National Center
142 Bull St.
Savannah, GA 31401
912-233-4501

Kentucky Governor's
   Mansion
Capital Ave.
Frankfort, KY 40602
502-564-3449

McFaddin-Ward House
1906 McFaddin Ave.
Beaumont, TX 77701
409-832-1906

Marjorie Kinnan Rawlings
   State Historic Site
Cross Creek
Route 3, Box 92
Hawthorne, FL 32640
904-466-3672

Maymont
1700 Hampton St.
Richmond, VA 23220
804-358-7166

Mississippi Governor's
   Mansion
300 East Capitol
Jackson, MS 39201
601-359-3175

Mississippi State Capitol
400 High St.
Jackson, MS 39205
601-359-3114

Mordecai Square Historic
Society
1 Mimosa Dr.
Raleigh, NC 27604
919-834-4844

Montpelier
P.O. Box 67
Montpelier Station, VA
   22967
703-672-2728

Natchez Pilgrimage Tours
P.O. Box 347
Natchez, MS 39121
1-800-647-6742

Old Blandford Church
319 S. Crater Rd.
Petersburg, VA 23804
804-733-2400

Old Salem
Winston-Salem, NC 27108
1-800-331-7018 (outside
   NC)

Pebble Hill
(U.S. Hwy. 319)
P.O. Box 830
Thomasville, GA 31799
912-226-2344

Pemberton House
11 7th St.
Columbus, GA 31901
706-323-7979

Point of Honor
Cabell St.
Lynchburg, VA 24505
804-847-1459

Reynolda House Museum
   of American Art
Reynolda Rd.
Winston-Salem, NC
27116
919-725-5325

Ringling Museum of Art
5401 Bay Shore Rd.
Sarasota, FL 34243
813-355-5101

Rockwood Museum
610 Shipley Rd.
Wilmington, DE 19809
302-571-7776

Rosedown
U.S. 61
St. Francisville, LA 70775
504-635-3332

Sherwood Forest
Rte. 5
Charles City, VA 23030
804-829-5377

Shirley Plantation
Rte. 5
Charles City, VA 23030
800-232-1613

The Old Court House
    Museum
1008 Cherry St.
Vicksburg, MS 39181
601-636-0741

Thomas Wolfe Memorial
48 Spruce St.
Asheville, NC 28807
704-253-8304

Virginia House
4301 Sulgrave Rd.
Richmond, VA 23221
804-353-4251

Walnut Grove Plantation
1200 Ott's Shoal Rd.
Roebuck, SC 29376
803-576-6546

Wilton Museum House
South Wilton Rd.
Richmond, VA 23226
804-282-5936

Bayou Sara
217 B Ferdinand
St. Francisiville, LA 70775
504-635-5446
*A catalog lists spices, hot
sauces, gumbo mixes,
mustards, seasonings, and
so forth*

Festival Flags
322 West Broad St.
Richmond, VA 23220
800-233-5247
For ever-welcoming flags

Fisherman's Cove
3201 Williams Blvd.
Kenner, LA 70065
800-443-3474.
*For a list of fresh crawfish,
Gulf shrimp, shipped daily,
liquid crab boil, and other
Louisiana specialties*

Florida Strawberry Festival
P.O. Drawer 1869
Plant City, FL 33564
813-752-9194

Fort Bend County Fair
P.O. Box 428
Rosenberg, TX 77471

Gambino's Bakeries
3609 Toledano St.
New Orleans, LA 70125
800-426-2466
*For a list of Mardi Gras
pastries and other specialities*

Irene's Beaten Biscuits
    Campbell's Restaurant
519 Main St.
Paris, KY 40361
606-987-5164
*They supply the Governor's
Mansion with beaten biscuits*

Mobile Department of
    Tourism
P.O. Box 1827
Mobile, AL
800-252-3862
*For Mardi Gras dates and
activities*

Peanut Patch, Inc.
P.O. Box 186
Courtland, VA 23837
800-544-0896
*The Jefferson Hotel uses only
these peanuts*

Plantation Lights
LA Highway 1
Baton Rouge, LA 70826
800-654-9701

Rohm's
8333 Maple
New Orleans, LA 70118
504-861-3611
*For beautiful Mardi Gras
wreaths, ribbons, candles*

St. Claire Ices
140 Walter St.
S. Norwalk, CT 06854
203-853-4774
*For ice creams to "South-
ernize" your next party*

Virginia First Thanks-
    giving Festival
P.O. Box 5132
Richmond, VA 23220

Photo Credits

Endpapers pattern adapted from an 18th-century wallpaper, courtesy of Scalamandre Silks; Half title illustration by Patsy Dreher, page i; Bob Donnan, page 81 (bottom); John Caleb Schwartz, page 80; Gene Burch, page 143; Sharon Squibb, page 78; Larry Sherwood, page 40 (left); Emyl Jenkins, pages 79, 93, 135, 141, 158, 164, 176; Colonial Williamsburg, page 20; Dan Loftin, page 13 (top).

In addition to the credits in the text, these credits are gratefully acknowledged:

Beacon Restaurant, 97; Berkeley Plantation, 76, 77; Bluff Hall 2; Butler Greenwood, 34, 48, 83; Colonial Williamsburg, 20, 80; Cross Creek, 86, 136, 138; Danville Museum (Last Capitol of the Confederacy), 23; Elgin, 53, 73; Fearrington Inn, 81; Fort Bend County Fair, 96; Governor's Mansion, Jackson, Mississippi, 21;

Grace Episcopal Church, St. Francisiville, 184; Houmas House, 5, 80; James Walker Homestead, 11, 94, 95; Kirkwood, 10, 54; Linden, 53, 83; McFaddin Ward, 67; James Morton, 81; Natchez Pilgrimage, 5, 62; Old Blandford Church, Petersburg, Virginia, 24; Pebble Hill, 62, 93, 139; Pemberton House, 54; Peter Patout, 52, 153; Rosedown Plantation, 185; Salem Tavern, 11, 46; Seven Sisters, 184; Sher-

wood Forest, 83; Shirley Plantation, 20, 21, 83, 156; Southern Maryland Decorator Show House, Newburg, MD, 8; Squibb Farm, Sulphur Springs, TN, 78; St. Augustine, FL, 14; Susina, 10, 83, 114; The Breakers, 98, 187; The Elms, 5, 11, 52, 55; The Homestead, 187; Thomas Wolfe Memorial, 5, 10; Tom Gray, 53; Walnut Grove, 139, 156; Walnut Hill, 138; Wilton 175; Winkler Bakery, Old Salem, 46.

Index